WORDPERFECT® 6.1 FOR WINDOWS® FOR DUMMIES®

2ND EDITION

Quick Reference

by Greg Harvey

IDG BOOKS
WORLDWIDE

IDG Books Worldwide, Inc.
An International Data Group Company

Foster City, CA ♦ Chicago, IL ♦ Indianapolis, IN ♦ Braintree, MA ♦ Dallas, TX

WordPerfect® 6.1 For Windows® For Dummies® Quick Reference, 2nd Edition

Published by
IDG Books Worldwide, Inc.
An International Data Group Company
919 E. Hillsdale Blvd.
Suite 400
Foster City, CA 94404

Library of Congress Catalog Card No.: 94-79830

ISBN: 1-56884-966-4

Printed in the United States of America

10 9 8 7 6 5

2A/RV/RS/ZV

Distributed in the United States by IDG Books Worldwide, Inc.

Distributed by Macmillan Canada for Canada; by Computer and Technical Books for the Caribbean Basin; by Contemporanea de Ediciones for Venezuela; by Distribuidora Cuspide for Argentina; by CITEC for Brazil; by Ediciones ZETA S.C.R. Ltda. for Peru; by Editorial Limusa SA for Mexico; by Transworld Publishers Limited in the United Kingdom and Europe; by Al-Maiman Publishers & Distributors for Saudi Arabia; by Simron Pty. Ltd. for South Africa; by IDG Communications (HK) Ltd. for Hong Kong; by Toppan Company Ltd. for Japan; by Addison Wesley Publishing Company for Korea; by Longman Singapore Publishers Ltd. for Singapore, Malaysia, Thailand, and Indonesia; by Unalis Corporation for Taiwan; by WS Computer Publishing Company, Inc. for the Philippines; by WoodsLane Pty. Ltd. for Australia; by WoodsLane Enterprises Ltd. for New Zealand.

For general information on IDG Books Worldwide's books in the U.S., please call our Consumer Customer Service department at 800-762-2974. For reseller information, including discounts and premium sales, please call our Reseller Customer Service department at 800-434-3422.

For information on where to purchase IDG Books Worldwide's books outside the U.S., contact IDG Books Worldwide at 415-655-3021 or fax 415-655-3295.

For information on translations, contact Marc Jeffrey Mikulich, Director, Foreign & Subsidiary Rights, at IDG Books Worldwide, 415-655-3018 or fax 415-655-3295.

For sales inquiries and special prices for bulk quantities, write to the address above or call IDG Books Worldwide at 415-655-3200.

For information on using IDG Books Worldwide's books in the classroom, or ordering examination copies, contact Jim Kelly at 800-434-2086.

For authorization to photocopy items for corporate, personal, or educational use, please contact Copyright Clearance Center, 222 Rosewood Drive, Danvers, MA 01923, or fax 508-750-4470.

is a trademark under exclusive license to IDG Books Worldwide, Inc., from International Data Group, Inc.

About the Author

Greg Harvey, the author of more than 45 computer books (and he just keeps on going and going and going . . .), has been training businesspeople in the use of IBM PC, DOS, Windows, and software applications programs, such as Word, Excel, WordPerfect, Lotus 1-2-3, and dBASE, since 1983. He has written numerous training manuals, user guides, and books for business users of software. Harvey is the author of *Excel for Windows 95 For Dummies, 1-2-3 For Dummies, More Excel 5 for Windows for Dummies, PC World WordPerfect 6 Handbook, DOS For Dummies Quick Reference, WordPerfect For Dummies Quick Reference,* and *Windows 95 For Dummies Quick Reference,* all from IDG Books.

Welcome to the world of IDG Books Worldwide.

IDG Books Worldwide, Inc., is a subsidiary of International Data Group, the world's largest publisher of computer-related information and the leading global provider of information services on information technology. IDG was founded more than 25 years ago and now employs more than 7,700 people worldwide. IDG publishes more than 250 computer publications in 67 countries (see listing below). More than 70 million people read one or more IDG publications each month.

Launched in 1990, IDG Books Worldwide is today the #1 publisher of best-selling computer books in the United States. We are proud to have received 8 awards from the Computer Press Association in recognition of editorial excellence and three from Computer Currents' First Annual Readers' Choice Awards, and our best-selling ...For Dummies® series has more than 19 million copies in print with translations in 28 languages. IDG Books Worldwide, through a joint venture with IDG's Hi-Tech Beijing, became the first U.S. publisher to publish a computer book in the People's Republic of China. In record time, IDG Books Worldwide has become the first choice for millions of readers around the world who want to learn how to better manage their businesses.

Our mission is simple: Every one of our books is designed to bring extra value and skill-building instructions to the reader. Our books are written by experts who understand and care about our readers. The knowledge base of our editorial staff comes from years of experience in publishing, education, and journalism — experience which we use to produce books for the '90s. In short, we care about books, so we attract the best people. We devote special attention to details such as audience, interior design, use of icons, and illustrations. And because we use an efficient process of authoring, editing, and desktop publishing our books electronically, we can spend more time ensuring superior content and spend less time on the technicalities of making books.

You can count on our commitment to deliver high-quality books at competitive prices on topics you want to read about. At IDG Books Worldwide, we continue in the IDG tradition of delivering quality for more than 25 years. You'll find no better book on a subject than one from IDG Books Worldwide.

John J. Kilcullen

John Kilcullen
President and CEO
IDG Books Worldwide, Inc.

IDG Books Worldwide, Inc., is a subsidiary of International Data Group, the world's largest publisher of computer-related information and the leading global provider of information services on information technology. International Data Group publishes over 250 computer publications in 67 countries. Seventy million people read one or more International Data Group publications each month. International Data Group's publications include: **ARGENTINA:** Computerworld Argentina, GamePro, Infoworld, PC World Argentina; **AUSTRALIA:** Australian Macworld, Client/Server Journal, Computer Living, Computerworld, Digital News, Network World, PC World, Publishing Essentials, Reseller; **AUSTRIA:** Computerwelt, PC TEST; **BELARUS:** PC World Belarus; **BELGIUM:** Data News; **BRAZIL:** Annuário de Informática, Computerworld Brazil, Connections, Super Game Power, Macworld, PC World Brazil, Publish Brazil, SUPERGAME; **BULGARIA:** Computerworld Bulgaria, Networkworld/Bulgaria, PC & MacWorld Bulgaria; **CANADA:** CIO Canada, ComputerWorld Canada, InfoCanada, Network World Canada, Reseller World; **CHILE:** Computerworld Chile, GamePro, PC World Chile; **COLUMBIA:** Computerworld Colombia, GamePro, PC World Colombia; **COSTA RICA:** PC World Costa Rica/Nicaragua; **THE CZECH AND SLOVAK REPUBLICS:** Computerworld Czechoslovakia, Elektronika Czechoslovakia, PC World Czechoslovakia; **DENMARK:** Communications World, Computerworld Danmark, Macworld Danmark, PC World Danmark, PC World Danmark Supplements, TECH World; **DOMINICAN REPUBLIC:** PC World Republica Dominicana; **ECUADOR:** PC World Ecuador, GamePro; **EGYPT:** Computerworld Middle East, PC World Middle East; **EL SALVADOR:** PC World Centro America; **FINLAND:** MikroPC, Tietoverkko, Tietoviikko; **FRANCE:** Distributique, Golden, Info PC, Le Guide du Monde Informatique, Le Monde Informatique, Reseaux & Telecoms; **GERMANY:** Computer Business, Computerwoche, Computerwoche Extra, Computerwoche Focus, Electronic Entertainment, GamePro, I/M Information Management, Macwelt, PC Welt; **GREECE:** GamePro, Macworld & Publish; **GUATEMALA:** PC World Centro America; **HONDURAS:** PC World Centro America; **HONG KONG:** Computerworld Hong Kong, PCWorld Hong Kong, Publish in Asia; **HUNGARY:** ABCD CD-ROM, Computerworld Szamitastechnika, PC & Mac World Hungary, PC-X Magazine; **INDIA:** Computerworld India, PC World India, Publish in Asia; **INDONESIA:** InfoKomputer PC World, Komputek Computerworld, Publish in Asia; **IRELAND:** ComputerScope, PC Live!; **ISRAEL:** PC World 32 BIT, People & Computers; **ITALY:** Computerworld Italia, Computerworld Italia Special Editions, Lotus Italia, Macworld Italia, Networking Italia, PC Shopping, PC World Italia, PC World/Walt Disney; **JAPAN:** Macworld Japan, Nikkei Personal Computing, SunWorld Japan, Windows World Japan; **KENYA:** East African Computer News; **KOREA:** Hi-Tech Information/Computerworld, Macworld Korea, PC World Korea; **MACEDONIA:** PC World Macedonia; **MALAYSIA:** Computerworld Malaysia, PC World Malaysia, Publish in Asia; **MEXICO:** Computerworld Mexico, GamePro, Macworld, PC World Mexico; **MYANMAR:** PC World Myanmar; **NETHERLANDS:** Computable, Computer! Totaal, LAN Magazine, Macworld, Net Magazine; **NEW ZEALAND:** Computer Buyer, Computerworld New Zealand, MTB, Network World, PC World New Zealand; **NICARAGUA:** PC World Costa Rica/Nicaragua; **NIGERIA:** PC World Africa; **NORWAY:** Computerworld Norge, Computerworld Privat, CW Rapport Klient/Tjener, CW Rapport Nettverk & Telecom, CW Rapport Offentlig Sektor, IDG's KURSGUIDE, Macworld Norge, Multimedia World, PC World Ekspress, PC World Netterverk, PC World Norge, PC World's Produktguide, Windows Spesial; **PAKISTAN:** Computerworld Pakistan, PC World Pakistan; **PANAMA:** GamePro, PC World Panama; **PARAGUAY:** PC World Paraguay; **P. R. OF CHINA:** China Computerworld, China Infoworld, Computer & Communication Electronic Product World, Electronics Today, Game Camp, PC World China, Popular Computer Week, Software World, Telecom Product World; **PERU:** Computerworld Peru, GamePro, PC World Profesional Peru, PC World Peru; **POLAND:** Computerworld Poland, Computerworld Special Report, Macworld, Networld, PC World Komputer; **PHILIPPINES:** Computerworld Philippines, PC Digest, Publish in Asia; **PORTUGAL:** Cerebro/PC World, Correio Informático/Computerworld, Mac•In/PC•In Portugal; **PUERTO RICO:** PC World Puerto Rico; **ROMANIA:** Computerworld Romania, PC World Romania, Telecom Romania; **RUSSIA:** Computerworld Rossiya, Network World Russia, PC World Russia, SINGAPORE:** Computerworld Singapore, PC World Singapore, Publish in Asia; **SLOVENIA:** MONITOR; **SOUTH AFRICA:** Computing S.A., Network World S.A., Software World; **SPAIN:** Computerworld España, COMUNICACIONES WORLD, Dealer World, Macworld España, PC World España; **SWEDEN:** CAP&Design, Computer Sweden, Corporate Computing, MacWorld, Maxi Data, MikroDatorn, Nätverk & Kommunikation, PC/Aktiv, PC World, Windows World; **SWITZERLAND:** Computerworld Schweiz, Macworld Schweiz, PCtip; **TAIWAN:** Computerworld Taiwan, Macworld Taiwan, PC World Taiwan, Publish Taiwan, Windows World; **THAILAND:** Thai Computerworld, Publish in Asia; **TURKEY:** Computerworld Monitor, MACWORLD Türkiye, PC WORLD Turkiye; **UKRAINE:** Computerworld Kiev, Computers & Software Magazine, PC World Ukraine; **UNITED KINGDOM:** Acorn User, Amiga Action, Amiga Computing, Amiga, Appletalk, CD Powerplay, CD-ROM Now, Computing, Connexion, GamePro, Lotus Magazine, Macaction, Macworld, Open Computing, Parents and Computers, PC Home, PC Works, The WEB; **UNITED STATES:** Cable in the Classroom, CD Review, CIO Magazine, Computerworld, Computerworld Client/Server Journal, Digital Video Magazine, DOS World, Electronic, InfoWorld, I-Way, Macworld, Maximize, MULTIMEDIA WORLD, Network World, PC World, PUBLISH, SWATPro Magazine, Video Event, WebMaster; **URUGUAY:** PC World Uruguay; **VENEZUELA:** Computerworld Venezuela, GamePro, PC World Venezuela; and **VIETNAM:** PC World Vietnam   10/17/95

Acknowledgments

I want to thank the following people, who worked so hard to make this book a reality:

David Solomon and John Kilcullen, for their support for this "baby" ...*For Dummies* book.

Brandon Nordin and Milissa Koloski, for coming up with the original concept of quick references for the rest of us.

Megg Bonar, for not once, but twice driving all the way out to the Inverness boonies to get me the WordPerfect 6.1 beta software.

Diane Steele, Kristin Cocks, Pam Mourouzis, Bill Helling, and Jennifer Wallis, for their editorial assistance.

Valerie Promise, for the technical review, and Beth Jenkins and the staff in Production.

Shane Gearing, for giving up his entire weekend to reshoot almost every single one of the figures in this second edition.

Jane Vait, for proofreading my lovely prose and checking over the thousand details in the manuscript.

Last, but never least, I want to acknowledge my indebtedness to Dan Gookin, whose vision, sardonic wit, and (sometimes) good humor produced *DOS For Dummies*, the "Mother" of all ...*For Dummies* books. Thanks for the inspiration and the book that made it all possible, Dan.

> Greg Harvey
> Inverness, California
> September, 1994

(The publisher would like to thank Patrick J. McGovern, without whom this book would not have been possible.)

Table of Contents

Introduction

Welcome to the *WordPerfect 6.1 For Windows For Dummies Quick Reference,* 2nd Edition, a quick reference that looks at the lighter side of WordPerfect commands (such as it is). I mean, how many ways does one person need to get to the same dialog box???

As a means of ferreting out the best possible paths to all the commands, features, and functions in WordPerfect for Windows, I offer you the *WordPerfect 6.1 For Windows For Dummies Quick Reference,* 2nd Edition. This book not only gives you the lowdown on WordPerfect commands, it also rates commands with icons indicating their suitability as well as their general safety (see the section "The cast of icons," later in this introduction, for a sneak preview).

For your convenience, this book isn't divided into any sections at all! All the commands are listed in alphabetical order, from Abbreviations to Zoom.

Each command is handled in a similar way. Below the command name, replete with its suitability and safety icons, you'll find a brief description of its function. If this description reads like stereo instructions, recheck the suitability icon: this command is probably not in your league.

Following the description come the sections that describe the path you take to accomplish the task. For each of the steps, you'll find a "picturesque" trail to follow and the name of each command and option you need to choose. In some cases, you'll encounter "For keyboard kronies" and "For mouse maniacs" sections — you choose which information you need!

Bringing up the rear, you'll find a "More stuff" section where I stick in any tips, warnings, reminders, or other trivia that just might come in handy when you use the command.

How do I use this book?

You have all heard of on-line help. Well, just think of this book as on-side help. Keep it by your side when you're at the computer, and before you try to use a WordPerfect command that you're the least bit unsure of, look up the command in the appropriate section. Scan the entry and look for any warnings (those bomb icons). Follow the sections "Pull-down menus," "For keyboard kronies," or "For mouse maniacs" to guide you through the options.

The cast of icons

In your travels with the WordPerfect for Windows commands in this book, you'll come across the following icons:

Something brand-new in version 6.1 of WordPerfect for Windows.

Recommended for your average WordPerfect user.

Not recommended for your average WordPerfect user.

Not suitable for your average WordPerfect user, but you may get stuck having to use this command anyway.

Safe for your data.

Generally safe in most circumstances unless you really don't follow instructions; then look out!

Potentially dangerous to data but necessary in the scheme of things. Be very careful — better yet, get somebody else to do it for you.

Safe only in the hands of a programmer or some other techy person. Stay clear unless you sign a release form and get hazard pay.

A tip to make you a more clever WordPerfect user.

Look out! There's some little something in this command that can get you into trouble (even when it's rated safe or generally safe).

Just a little note to remind you of some trivia or other that may someday save your bacon.

Flags cross references to other areas of this book that might be of interest to you.

A handy-dandy guide to point you straight to the sections in *WordPerfect 6.1 For Windows For Dummies* where you can find more examples of how to use this command.

Features of WordPerfect 6.1 for Windows

Abbreviations

Lets you define an abbreviation for some stock text you use; when you type the abbreviation and press Ctrl+A, WordPerfect for Windows expands the abbreviation to its correct size. If you work for the firm Branwurst and Bagel, for example, you can type **bb** and press Ctrl+A, and — presto! — the program inserts *Branwurst and Bagel* into the document.

Pull-down menu

```
Create and expand abbreviations
File  Edit  View  Insert  Format  Table  Graphics  Tools  Window  Help
        Bullets & Numbers...
        Character...          Ctrl+W
Times New Roman  12           1.0  Tables        Columns     91%
        Abbreviations...
        Date                    ▶
        Other                   ▶

        Footnote                ▶
        Endnote                 ▶

        Comment                 ▶
        Sound...
        Bookmark...

        Spreadsheet/Database    ▶
        File...
        Object...
        Acquire Image...
        Select Image Source...

        Page Break    Ctrl+Enter

Insert        HP LaserJet 4 Plus/4M Plus (Win)    Select  November 18, 1994  5:37PM  Pg 1 Ln 1" Pos 1"
```

For keyboard kronies

To expand an abbreviation, press

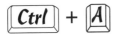

$Ctrl$ + A

Using abbreviations

To create an abbreviation, follow these steps:

1. Type the text you want to assign an abbreviation to and then select (highlight) the text.

2. Choose <u>A</u>bbreviations from the <u>I</u>nsert pull-down menu.

3. Choose C̲reate to display the Create Abbreviation dialog box.

4. Type the abbreviation you want to assign to the selected text in the A̲bbreviation Name text box and then choose OK or press Enter.

5. Choose C̲lose in the Abbreviations dialog box.

After you create an abbreviation, you can use it by typing the abbreviation in the document and then pressing Ctrl+A to expand it.

More stuff

If you're into toolbars, you can create a button that inserts stock text into a document when you click the button. To do so, create a Play A K̲eyboard Script button and then type the text you want entered each time you click your custom button on the toolbar (see the "Toolbars" section).

Advance

Positions text precisely on the page without requiring you to monkey around with tabs, spaces, and hard returns.

Pull-down menus

The Advance dialog box

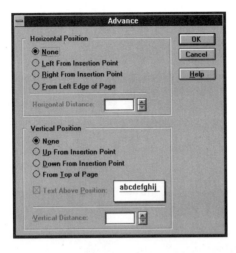

Option or Button	*Function*
Horizontal Position	
None	Does not adjust the horizontal position one iota (the default)
Left From Insertion Point	Adjusts, by the amount you specify, the printing of the text that follows to the left of the insertion point's current position
Right From Insertion Point	Adjusts, by the amount you specify, the printing of the text that follows to the right of the insertion point's current position
From Left Edge of Page	Adjusts the text that follows by a fixed amount from the left edge of the page
Horizontal Distance	Specifies the amount to adjust the text according to which Horizontal Position radio button you have selected
Vertical Position	
None	Does not adjust the vertical position one iota (the default)

(continued)

Option or Button	*Function*
<u>U</u>p From Insertion Point	Adjusts, by the amount you specify, the printing of the text that follows upward from the insertion point's current position
<u>D</u>own From Insertion Point	Adjusts, by the amount you specify, the printing of the text that follows downward from the insertion point's current position
From <u>T</u>op of Page	Adjusts the text that follows by a fixed amount from the top edge of the page
Text Above <u>P</u>osition	With the From <u>T</u>op of Page option on, places the first line of advanced text above the position as calculated from the top of the page; with the From <u>T</u>op of Page option off, places the first line of text below this vertical advance position
<u>V</u>ertical Distance	Specifies the amount to adjust the text according to which Vertical Position radio button you select

More stuff

When you're using the Advance feature to position text, you can use both a Horizontal and a Vertical option if necessary. Before you use this command, always be sure to position the insertion point ahead of the first character you want advanced on the page.

For more information about this command, see Chapter 19 of *WordPerfect For Windows For Dummies.*

Bar Code

Lets you add a POSTNET (*Post*al *N*umeric *E*ncoding *T*echnique) bar code when you're addressing an envelope or creating a mailing label. A *bar code* is that funny-looking computer script that resembles the one food stores use to mark grocery items — which the scanners can never read. Using bar codes in your mailing addresses can save you some bucks with the post office, however, so they're worth using.

Pull-down menus

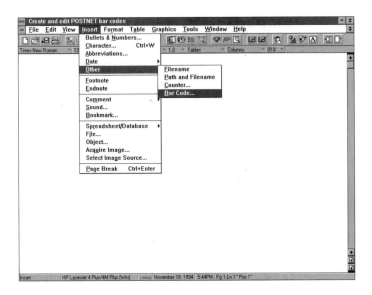

Belly up to the bar (code)

To insert a bar code in an address (or elsewhere in a document if you're really inclined), follow these steps:

1. Position the insertion point where you want the bar code to appear.

2. Choose Other from the Insert pull-down menu and then choose Bar code.

3. Type the 11-digit Delivery Point Bar Code, 9-digit ZIP + 4, or 5-digit ZIP Code in the POSTNET Bar Code dialog box.

4. Press Enter or choose OK.

When you return to your document, you see the weird bar-code characters in the document.

More stuff

To decipher a bar code you have inserted in a document, open the Reveal Codes window by pressing Alt+F3. WordPerfect for Windows displays the [Bar Code] secret code, which lists the digits in English as soon as you select it. To get rid of a bar code, remove the [Bar Code] secret code from the Reveal Codes window: either select it, drag it out (kicking and screaming), and drop it anywhere outside the Reveal Codes window or zap it with the Delete key.

You can also add POSTNET bar codes to envelopes when you're addressing them with the nifty, new Envelope feature (see the "Envelope" section).

For more information about this command, see Chapter 19 of *WordPerfect For Windows For Dummies*.

Block Protect (see "Keep Text Together")

Bold

Prints selected text in boldface type.

For keyboard kronies

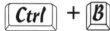

For mouse maniacs

Click **b** on the WordPerfect 6.1 for Windows toolbar.

Would you be so bold . . .

To make a section of text bold, follow these steps:

1. Select (highlight) the text you want to be bold.

2. Click the Bold button on the WordPerfect 6.1 for Windows toolbar (see "For mouse maniacs" in this section) or press Ctrl+B.

To make a section of text bold as you type it, follow these steps:

1. Position the insertion point at the place where you want the first bold character to appear.

2. Click the Bold button on the WordPerfect 6.1 for Windows toolbar (see "For mouse maniacs" in this section) or press Ctrl+B. When you boldface a section of text, WordPerfect for Windows inserts the secret codes [Bold><Bold] with the insertion point between them.

3. Type the text you want to appear in bold.

4. Turn off bold by clicking the Bold button on the Power bar, pressing Ctrl+B, or pressing → once to move beyond the ⟨Bold] secret code that turns off bold.

More stuff

To get rid of bold in text, open the Reveal Codes window and delete either the [Bold> or <Bold] code that encloses the text.

For more information about this command, see Chapter 8 of *WordPerfect For Windows For Dummies*.

Bookmark

Marks your place in a document so that you can get right back to that location when you want to.

Pull-down menu

```
Set, rename, and go to bookmarks
 File  Edit  View  Insert  Format  Table  Graphics  Tools  Window  Help
                   Bullets & Numbers...
                   Character...        Ctrl+W
Times New Roman   Abbreviations...              1.0   Tables      Columns      91%
                   Date              ▶
                   Other             ▶
                   Footnote          ▶
                   Endnote           ▶
                   Comment           ▶
                   Sound...
                   Bookmark...
                   Spreadsheet/Database ▶
                   File...
                   Object...
                   Acquire Image...
                   Select Image Source...
                   Page Break     Ctrl+Enter
Insert        HP LaserJet 4 Plus/4M Plus (Win)   Select November 18, 1994  5.45PM  Pg 1 Ln 1" Pos 1"
```

For keyboard kronies

To find a QuickMark, press

Ctrl + **Q**

To set a QuickMark, press

Ctrl + **Shift** + **Q**

The Bookmark dialog box

Option or Button	Function
Bookmark List	Lists all the bookmarks you have defined for the document
Go To	Locates the bookmark you have highlighted in the Bookmark List box
Close	Closes the Bookmark dialog box without selecting any of the bookmark options
Go To & Select	Locates and marks as a block the bookmark you have highlighted in the Bookmark List box; you must list the bookmark as a Selected type to make this option available
Create	Opens the Create Bookmark dialog box, in which you can name your new bookmark

Option or Button	*Function*
Move	Relocates the bookmark you have highlighted in the Bookmark List box to the current position of the insertion point in the document
Rename	Opens the Rename Bookmark dialog box, in which you can change the name of the bookmark you have highlighted in the Bookmark List box
Delete	Deletes the bookmark you have highlighted in the Bookmark List box after your confirmation
Set QuickMark	Sets the QuickMark bookmark at the insertion point's position
Find QuickMark	Moves the insertion point to the location of the QuickMark bookmark in your document

Creating a bookmark

To create a bookmark, follow these steps:

1. Position the insertion point at the beginning of the text where you want the bookmark placed. To create a Selected bookmark, select all the text you want to be highlighted when you click Go To & Select in the Bookmark dialog box.

2. Choose Bookmark from the Insert pull-down menu and choose Create to display the Create Bookmark dialog box.

3. To name your bookmark, edit the selected text displayed in the Bookmark Name text box (or use as the bookmark name the text that you copied from the document verbatim).

4. Choose OK or press Enter to return to your document.

Finding a bookmark

To find a bookmark, follow these steps:

1. Choose Bookmark from the Insert pull-down menu.

2. Choose the name of the bookmark you want to find by using the Bookmark List box.

3. To position the insertion point at the beginning of the bookmark, choose Go To. To also select the bookmark text, choose Go To & Select instead. (Hey, the Go To & Select button works only if the bookmark type is listed as Selected.)

A bookmark for those in a hurry

QuickMark is the name of a special bookmark you set at the insertion point simply by pressing Ctrl+Shift+Q. To return to the QuickMark, you simply press Ctrl+Q.

If you want, you can have WordPerfect for Windows automatically set the QuickMark at the insertion point's current position every time you save a document. By doing so, you can save and set the QuickMark at the end of a work session, open the document the next day, and press Ctrl+Q to find the place you were last working (now that's quick!).

To have WordPerfect for Windows set the QuickMark every time you save your document, choose Preferences from the Edit menu and then choose Environment in the Preferences dialog box. These steps open the Environment Preferences dialog box, where you put an X in the check box for Set QuickMark On Save.

More stuff

You can always delete a bookmark you no longer want by using Delete in the Bookmark dialog box. You can also delete a bookmark quickly by removing the [Bookmark] secret code from the Reveal Codes window: select it and drag it out (kicking and screaming) or zap it with the Delete key.

For more information about this command, see Chapter 25 of *WordPerfect For Windows For Dummies*.

Borders

Lets you put a border around paragraphs, pages, or columns in your document.

Pull-down menus

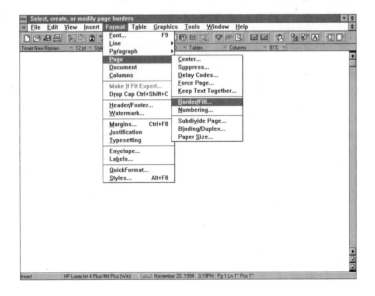

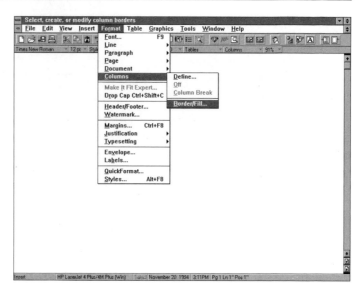

South of the border . . .

WordPerfect for Windows makes it a snap to create a border
around paragraphs and pages or between the columns of your
document. To create a border, follow these steps:

1. Position the insertion point in the paragraph, on the page,
   or between the columns where you want the borders to
   begin.

2. Choose P̲aragraph, P̲age, or C̲olumns from the Fo̲rmat pull-
   down menu and then choose the B̲order/Fill command from
   the cascading menu.

3. Choose a border style by clicking the button to the right of
   B̲order Style and then choosing a border style from the
   pop-up palette or by choosing the name of the border from
   the drop-down list box.

4. To choose a fill pattern for the borders, either click the button to the right of <u>F</u>ill Style and then choose the fill style from the pop-up palette or choose the name of the border from the drop-down list box.

5. Choose OK or press Enter.

How do you turn off these confounded borders?!

When you add paragraph, page, or column borders to a document, by default the Apply Border to Current Paragraph, Page, Column check box is enabled. If you disable this option, WordPerfect for Windows gets carried away and adds these borders to all subsequent paragraphs, pages, or columns in that document. You can turn off these borders, however, by positioning the insertion point in the first paragraph, page, or column that should *not* have a border and opening the appropriate Border dialog box. Then choose <None> as the border style.

More stuff

If you know that you want a border around only a particular paragraph or group of paragraphs, either leave the X in the default Apply Border to Current Paragraph, Page, Column check box in the dialog box or select those paragraphs before adding the paragraph borders. This way, you don't have to go through the nonsense of turning off the paragraph borders.

For more information about this command, see Chapter 16 of *WordPerfect For Windows For Dummies.*

Bullets and Numbers

Makes it incredibly simple to create bulleted or numbered lists in your document.

Pull-down menu

For keyboard kronies

To insert another bullet or the next number, press

Ctrl + **Shift** + **B**

For mouse maniacs

Click ⊞ on the WordPerfect 6.1 for Windows toolbar to insert another bullet.

Bullets and numbers in a snap

To create a numbered or bulleted list in a document, follow these steps:

1. Position the insertion point at the beginning of the first line on which you want to create a bullet or number.

2. Choose Bullets & Numbers from the Insert pull-down menu to open the Bullets & Numbers dialog box.

3. Choose from the Styles list box the type of bullet or style of numbering you want to use.

4. To choose a fill pattern for the borders, either click the button to the right of <u>F</u>ill Style and then choose the fill style from the pop-up palette or choose the name of the border from the drop-down list box.

5. Choose OK or press Enter.

How do you turn off these confounded borders?!

When you add paragraph, page, or column borders to a document, by default the Apply Border to Current Paragraph, Page, Column check box is enabled. If you disable this option, WordPerfect for Windows gets carried away and adds these borders to all subsequent paragraphs, pages, or columns in that document. You can turn off these borders, however, by positioning the insertion point in the first paragraph, page, or column that should *not* have a border and opening the appropriate Border dialog box. Then choose <None> as the border style.

More stuff

 If you know that you want a border around only a particular paragraph or group of paragraphs, either leave the X in the default Apply Border to Current Paragraph, Page, Column check box in the dialog box or select those paragraphs before adding the paragraph borders. This way, you don't have to go through the nonsense of turning off the paragraph borders.

 For more information about this command, see Chapter 16 of *WordPerfect For Windows For Dummies.*

Bullets and Numbers

Makes it incredibly simple to create bulleted or numbered lists in your document.

Pull-down menu

```
Insert a variety of bullets and numbers into the document
 File   Edit   View   Insert   Format   Table   Graphics   Tools   Window   Help
                   Bullets & Numbers...
Times New Roman  12  Character...        Ctrl+W         1.0    Tables        Columns      91%
                   Abbreviations...
                   Date                        ►
                   Other                       ►
                   Footnote                    ►
                   Endnote                     ►
                   Comment
                   Sound...
                   Bookmark...
                   Spreadsheet/Database        ►
                   File...
                   Object...
                   Acquire Image...
                   Select Image Source...
                   Page Break      Ctrl+Enter

Insert       HP LaserJet 4 Plus/4M Plus (Win)   Select  November 18, 1994  5:45PM  Pg 1 Ln 1" Pos 1"
```

For keyboard kronies

To insert another bullet or the next number, press

Ctrl + **Shift** + **B**

For mouse maniacs

Click  on the WordPerfect 6.1 for Windows toolbar to insert another bullet.

Bullets and numbers in a snap

To create a numbered or bulleted list in a document, follow these steps:

1. Position the insertion point at the beginning of the first line on which you want to create a bullet or number.

2. Choose Bullets & Numbers from the Insert pull-down menu to open the Bullets & Numbers dialog box.

3. Choose from the Styles list box the type of bullet or style of numbering you want to use.

4. If you're using numbers and want to begin the numbering at a number other than one, choose Starting Value and enter the new start number in the text box.

5. If you want to insert another bullet or the next number simply by pressing Enter, choose New Bullet or Number on ENTER to place an X in its check box.

6. Choose OK or press Enter.

After you choose the bullet or numbering style, WordPerfect for Windows inserts the bullet or first number and indents the insertion point. After you type your first numbered or bulleted text, press Enter. If you chose the New Bullet or Number on ENTER option, the program automatically inserted another bullet or the next number in the text. If you did not choose this function, press Ctrl+Shift+B to insert another bullet or number.

More stuff

To turn off the automatic bulleting or numbering function, open the Bullet & Numbers dialog box and deselect the New Bullet or Number on ENTER option to remove the X from its check box.

For more information about this command, see Chapter 25 of *WordPerfect For Windows For Dummies.*

Button Bars (renamed Toolbars; see "Toolbars")

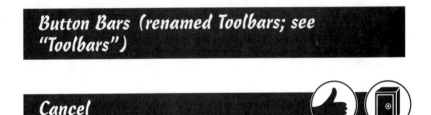

Cancel

Backs you out of pull-down menu commands and dialog box options or discontinues a procedure before you get yourself into real trouble!

For keyboard kronies

Esc

For mouse maniacs

To put away a pull-down menu, click the mouse pointer somewhere in the document. To put away a dialog box, click Cancel.

Center Line

Centers a line of text horizontally between the left and right margins.

Pull-down menus

For keyboard kronies

QuickMenus

Position the insertion point in front of the first character on the line to be centered. Click the secondary mouse button (the right button if you're a right-handed mouser, or the left button if you're a left-handed mouser) and choose Center from the QuickMenu.

Centering a line of text

To center a line before you type it, press Shift+F7 to move the insertion point to the center of the line. Then type your text and press Enter. After you press Enter, WordPerfect for Windows returns the insertion point to the left margin of the new line.

To center a line of existing text, put the insertion point at the beginning of the line and then press Shift+F7.

To center a bunch of lines, select (highlight) them and then press Shift+F7.

You can center text on a specific column position or tab stop on a line. To do so, press the spacebar or Tab key until you reach the place where you want to center the text and then press Shift+F7.

When you center a single line of text (either before or after you type it), WordPerfect for Windows inserts a [Hd Center on Marg] code in front of the first character and a [HRt] code after the last character. When you center a bunch of lines you have selected, the program encloses the lines in [Just> and <Just] codes, which turn center justification on and off.

To get rid of centering, open the Reveal Codes window by pressing Alt+F3. Delete the [Hd Center on Marg] code or the [Just> or <Just] code by clicking any code and dragging it out of the Reveal Codes window, pressing Backspace over any code, or placing the cursor to the left of the code and pressing Delete.

More stuff

You can also center text by changing the justification of a document from normal left justification to center justification. For more information about this method, see the "Justification" section.

Center Page

Centers text on a page vertically between the top and bottom margins.

Pull-down menus

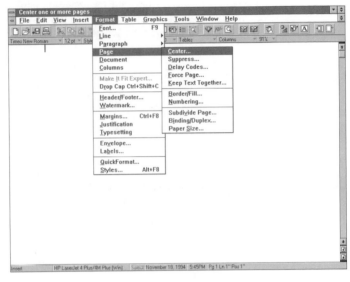

The Center Page(s) dialog box

Option or Button	Function
Current Page	Vertically centers just the text from the current page between the top and bottom margins
Current and Subsequent Pages	Vertically centers the current page page and all following pages
No Centering	The default setting; changes to Turn Centering Off after you have used the Current and Subsequent Pages radio button to turn vertical centering on

More stuff

When you choose the Current Page radio button, WordPerfect for Windows puts a [Cntr Cur Pg] secret code at the top of the page. When you choose the Current and Subsequent Pages radio button, the program puts a [Cntr Pgs] at the top of the current page.

Auto Code Placement automatically locates the secret code for centering pages at the top of the current page, regardless of where your insertion point is located on that page.

If you turn on vertical centering and nothing changes on-screen, WordPerfect for Windows is in draft view and you must change it to page view or two-page view.

For more information about this command, see Chapter 10 of *WordPerfect For Windows For Dummies.*

Close (Document)

Closes the current document window and prompts you to save the file, in case you're just about to blow some of your work away by forgetting to save before closing.

Pull-down menu

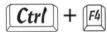

```
Close the current document window - Ctrl+F4
File  Edit  View  Insert  Format  Table  Graphics  Tools  Window  Help
New...          Ctrl+T
Open...         Ctrl+O
Close           Ctrl+F4
Save            Ctrl+S
Save As...      F3

Master Document      ▶
Compare Document     ▶
Document Summary...
Document Info...

Print...        Ctrl+P
Send            ▶

Exit            Alt+F4
```

Insert   HP LaserJet 4 Plus/4M Plus (Win)   Select November 18, 1994   5:47PM   Pg 1 Ln 1" Pos 1"

For keyboard kronies

 $Ctrl$ + $F4$

For mouse maniacs

Double-click the Control-menu button for the document window (it's the one immediately to the left of File on the pull-down menu).

More stuff

When you close a document that contains information that has not been saved, the program displays a warning dialog box that asks whether you want to save changes to your document. To save a document, choose Yes or press Enter. If a document has not been saved yet, the Save As dialog box appears and you have to name the document. (See the "Save As" section for more information.)

Coaches

These babies coach you through each step required to complete a lot of useful tasks, such as adding borders around paragraphs, creating columns, and using headers and footers.

Pull-down menu

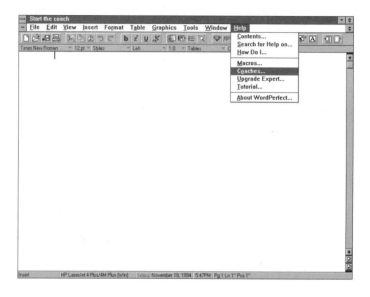

For mouse maniacs

Click on the WordPerfect 6.1 for Windows toolbar to open the Coaches dialog box.

The Coaches dialog box

```
┌──────────────────────────────────────────────────┐
│ ▭           Coaches                                │
│  Choose a coach to guide you through      ╔═══╗    │
│  the specified task.                      ╚═══╝    │
│  ┌──────────────────────────────────┬─┐  ┌──────┐ │
│  │ Bookmarks                        │▲│  │  OK  │ │
│  │ Borders - Columns                │ │  └──────┘ │
│  │ Borders - Page                   │ │  ┌──────┐ │
│  │ Borders - Paragraph              │ │  │Cancel│ │
│  │ Bulleted or Numbered Lists       │ │  └──────┘ │
│  │ Columns                          │ │  ┌──────┐ │
│  │ Endnotes                         │ │  │ Help │ │
│  │ Footnotes                        │ │  └──────┘ │
│  │ Graphics                         │ │           │
│  │ Headers and Footers              │▼│           │
│  └──────────────────────────────────┴─┘           │
│  Description:                                      │
│  ┌────────────────────────────────────────┐       │
│  │ ▨▨▨   Create or find Bookmarks and      │       │
│  │ ▨▨▨   QuickMarks.                       │       │
│  └────────────────────────────────────────┘       │
└──────────────────────────────────────────────────┘
```

How to get yourself some coaching

To use a coach, you simply open the Coaches dialog box (see the preceding figure) by choosing C̲oaches from the H̲elp pull-down menu. Then select the topic for which you want coaching in the Choose a coach to guide you through the specialized task list box and choose OK or press Enter. After selecting the topic you want coaching on, you are walked through a series of dialog boxes that explain the steps necessary to accomplish the chosen task. Depending upon the topic and the particular step at hand, you may find that your coach offers you a choice between a Continue and Quit Coach button or a Continue and a Show Me button. Click Show Me if you want to be prompted as you actually perform the task. Click Continue to move to the next step in the procedure. Click Quit Coach when you've had enough coaching for one day.

More stuff

Coaches represent but a small part of the on-line Help system built into WordPerfect for Windows. For much more on the help options at your disposal, see the "Help" section.

Columns

Enables you to lay out text in multiple columns. You can choose between newspaper columns, in which text flows up and down each column, and parallel columns, in which text flows across the page.

Pull-down menus

For keyboard kronies

To break a column and move the insertion point to the next column, press

Ctrl + *Enter*

For mouse maniacs

Click the Columns button on the Power bar and choose the
number of newspaper columns (up to five) you want to create at
the insertion point. To use the Columns button to turn off
newspaper columns later in the document, click it and then
choose the Columns Off command from the drop-down list.

To display and define your columns by using the Columns dialog
box, double-click the Columns button on the Power bar.

The Columns dialog box

Option or Button	Function
Number of Columns	Selects the Columns option, in which you enter the number of newspaper or parallel columns you want to create (between 2 and 32).
Type	Choose Newspaper when you want the text to be read up and down the columns across the page, Balanced Newspaper when you want WordPerfect for Windows to create even newspaper columns, Parallel when you want the text to read across and then down the columns, or Parallel w/Block Protect when you want parallel columns that always stay together on a page.

Option or Button	*Function*
Column Spacing	Use Spacing Between Columns to change the distance between the columns (0.500-inch by default). If you're creating parallel columns, you can use Line Spacing Between Rows In Parallel Columns to increase or decrease, in half-line increments, the number of lines between the parallel columns in your document.
Column Widths	Enables you to modify the width of and the space between specific newspaper or parallel columns. (By default, WordPerfect for Windows creates uniform columns with the same amount of space between them.) To change the width of a column, choose its text box and enter the width. To change the space between a particular pair of columns, choose its Space text box and enter the new distance.

Entering text in columns

You can enter text either before or after you create the columns. When you're using newspaper columns, you usually will find it easier to type the text first in normal single-column layout and then create the newspaper columns that reset the text. If you create newspaper columns before you type text, keep in mind that you may want to break a column early so that you can continue entering text at the top of the next column. To break the column, either press Ctrl+Enter or choose Columns from the Format pull-down menu followed by Column Break.

With parallel columns, you should define the columns before you type the text. After you complete an entry in one column, you have to insert a column break (by pressing Ctrl+Enter or choosing Columns from the Format pull-down menu followed by Column Break) to advance one column to the right. When you enter the text for the last column in that row, insert a column break to return the insertion point to the first parallel column in the next row. If you want to insert a blank column, insert two column breaks rather than just one.

Editing text in columns

When you create text columns in your document, the Status bar changes to include a *Col* indicator. This indicator tells you the column position of the insertion point. To move the insertion point between columns and edit their text, press Alt+→ to move one column to the right or Alt+← to move one column to the left.

You can also use the options in the Go To dialog box to move between columns (see the "Go To" section).

Getting your columns adjusted

You can adjust the width of your columns by using the ruler bar (see the "Ruler Bar" section).

To adjust the width of the columns, click and drag either the column margin icons on the tab ruler or the gray spacer between the columns.

More stuff

When you create columns, WordPerfect for Windows adds a [Col Def] secret code, which defines the type and number of columns and also turns them on. To get rid of columns and return to regular text, remove this code by clicking it and dragging it out of the Reveal Codes window, by pressing Backspace over it, or by placing your cursor to the left of the code and pressing Delete.

Rather than try to deal with parallel columns and their column breaks, try using tables instead (see the "Tables" section).

Tables are not only more versatile than parallel columns are but also are much easier to deal with.

For more information about this command, see Chapter 16 of *WordPerfect For Windows For Dummies.*

Comments

Adds comments to your text that appear in a text box on your screen but are not printed as part of the document.

Pull-down menus

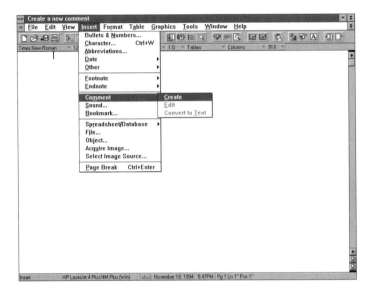

Creating a comment

To create a comment, follow these steps:

1. Place the insertion point in the document where you want the comment to be located.

2. Choose Comment from the Insert menu and choose Create from the cascading menu.

3. Type the text of your comment in the Comment editing window. To insert your name (as it appears in the User Info For Comments and Summary area of the Environment Preferences dialog box) in the comment, choose Name on the Comment feature bar. To insert the current date or time (or both) in the comment, choose Date or Time on the Comment feature bar.

4. When you create a comment, WordPerfect for Windows displays a comment icon in the left margin of the line that contains the comment. If you want to add your initials (as they appear in the User Info For Comments and Summary area of the Environment Preferences dialog box) to the comment text and have them appear in the comment icon, choose Initials on the Comment feature bar.

5. Apply any new fonts, font sizes, or attributes to the comment text by using the appropriate commands from the Format pull-down menu.

6. When the text of your comment looks the way you want it to look, choose Close to hide the Comment feature bar and return to the document window. WordPerfect for Windows then inserts a comment icon in the left margin of the line that contains the comment. To display the text of the comment (which appears as a balloon), click the comment icon. To hide the comment text balloon, click the mouse pointer again anywhere in the document.

Editing a comment

To edit a comment, either double-click the comment icon or click the comment icon or text balloon with the secondary mouse button (the right button if you're a right-handed mouser, or the left button if you're a left-handed mouser) and choose Edit from the QuickMenu. After you finish making your changes in the Comment editing window, choose Close on the Comment feature bar.

To get rid of a comment, click the comment icon or comment text balloon with the secondary mouse button and choose Delete from the QuickMenu.

More stuff

When you create a comment, WordPerfect for Windows inserts a [Comment] secret code at the insertion point's current position. You can also get rid of a comment by zapping this code in the Reveal Codes window.

For more information about this command, see Chapter 26 of *WordPerfect For Windows For Dummies*.

Conditional End of Page (See "Keep Text Together")

Convert Case

Changes the text you have selected to all uppercase, all lowercase, or initial capital letters.

Pull-down menus

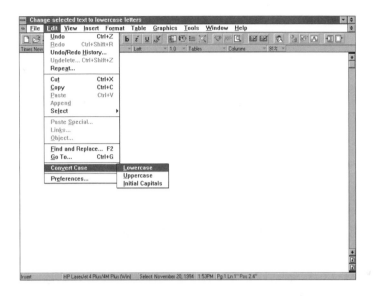

It's a simple case of conversion . . .

To convert the case of some text, select the text and choose
Convert Case from the Edit pull-down menu. Then choose the
convert command you want: Lowercase to convert all the letters
to lowercase, Uppercase to convert them all to uppercase, or
Initial Capitals to capitalize only the first letter of each word.

For more information about this command, see Chapter 8 of
WordPerfect For Windows For Dummies.

Cut, Copy, and Paste

Enables you to move or copy blocks of text within the same document or to different documents that are open in other document
windows.

Pull-down menu

```
Cut or move selected text or graphics to the Clipboard - Ctrl+X
File   Edit   View   Insert   Format   Table   Graphics   Tools   Window   Help
       Undo              Ctrl+Z
       Redo              Ctrl+Shift+R
       Undo/Redo History...
       Undelete... Ctrl+Shift+Z
       Repeat...

       Cut               Ctrl+X
       Copy              Ctrl+C
       Paste             Ctrl+V
       Append
       Select                      ▶

       Paste Special...
       Links...
       Object...

       Find and Replace... F2
       Go To...          Ctrl+G

       Convert Case                ▶

       Preferences...
```

```
Insert        HP LaserJet 4 Plus/4M Plus (Win)     Select  November 18, 1994  6:00PM  Pg 1 Ln 1" Pos 1.5"
```

For keyboard kronies

To cut the selected text to the Clipboard (defined in "Using Cut, Copy, and Paste" later in this section), press

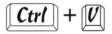

To copy the selected text to the Clipboard, press

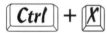

To paste the contents of the Clipboard at the insertion point's current position, press

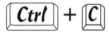

For mouse maniacs

Click ▨ on the WordPerfect 6.1 for Windows toolbar to cut the
selected text to the Clipboard (defined in the section "Using Cut,
Copy, and Paste").

Click ▨ on the WordPerfect 6.1 for Windows toolbar to copy the
selected text to the Clipboard.

Click ▨ on the WordPerfect 6.1 for Windows toolbar to paste the
contents of the Clipboard at the insertion point's current
position.

QuickMenus

To cut or copy a selection, click the selected text with the secondary mouse button (the right button if you're a right-handed
mouser, or the left button if you're a left-handed mouser) and
choose Cut or Copy from the QuickMenu.

To paste the contents of the Clipboard at the insertion point's
current position, click the secondary mouse button and choose
Paste from the QuickMenu.

Using Cut, Copy, and Paste

In WordPerfect for Windows (as in all other Windows programs),
the procedure for moving document text is called *cut and paste,*
and the procedure for copying text is called (what else?) *copy and
paste.* Both procedures use a special area of memory, called the
Clipboard, that temporarily holds the information to be moved or
copied.

When you use Cut, Copy, and Paste, keep in mind that the
Clipboard normally holds only one block of selected text at a
time. Any new text you copy to the Clipboard completely replaces
the text that is already there. The only way to add information to
the Clipboard is to use the Append command from the Edit pull-
down menu. The selected text you place in the Clipboard stays
there until you replace it or exit from WordPerfect for Windows;
you can use the Paste command from the Edit menu, however, to
copy the selected text over and over again in any document.

To move or copy text

To move text, first select it. Then cut the selection out of the document and copy it to the Clipboard by using one of three methods: choose Cut from the Edit pull-down menu, click on the WordPerfect 6.1 for Windows toolbar, or press Ctrl+X. To copy the selected text instead, either choose Copy from the Edit menu, click on the WordPerfect 6.1 for Windows toolbar, or press Ctrl+C.

To paste the cut or copied text elsewhere in the document, move the insertion point to where you want to insert the text. Then paste by choosing the Paste command from the Edit menu, clicking on the WordPerfect 6.1 for Windows toolbar, or pressing Ctrl+V.

More stuff

Keep in mind that you don't have to go through all the cut- or copy-and-paste rigmarole — you can also move or copy text with the good old drag-and-drop method (see the section "Drag and Drop (Text)" for details).

For more information about this command, see Chapter 6 of *WordPerfect For Windows For Dummies.*

Date

Puts today's date in your document either as text, which you must update yourself, or as a secret code, which WordPerfect for Windows updates every time you open the document.

Pull-down menu

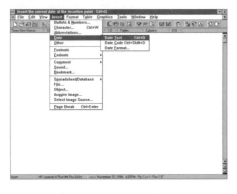

For keyboard kronies

To insert the date as text, press

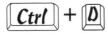

To insert the date as a code, press

Inserting the date as text

To insert the current date as text, which doesn't change unless you open the document and edit it, follow these steps:

1. Position the insertion point where you want the date to appear.

2. Choose Date from the Insert menu and choose Date Text or press Ctrl+D.

Inserting the date as a secret code

To insert the date as a secret code, which WordPerfect for Windows automatically keeps up-to-date for you, follow these steps:

1. Position the insertion point where you want to insert the secret date code. The date also appears here.

2. Choose Date from the Insert menu and choose Date Code or press Ctrl+Shift+D.

Selecting a new date format

1. Choose Date from the Insert menu and then choose Date Format to open the Document Date/Time Format dialog box.

2. Choose a sample format in the Predefined Format list box and then choose OK or press Enter.

More stuff

When you select the Date Code command, WordPerfect for Windows inserts the secret code [Date] in the text at the insertion point's position. If you choose a new date format, the program inserts [Date Fmt] in the document at the insertion point's position.

Choosing a new predefined date format has no effect on the dates you have already inserted in the text by using the Date Text and Date Code commands.

For more information about this command, see Chapter 9 of *WordPerfect For Windows For Dummies*.

Delete (Text)

WordPerfect for Windows provides loads of ways to get rid of text. The easiest way to delete text is to select the text (see the section "Select (Text)" for details) and then press Delete or Backspace.

QuickMenus

Select the text to be deleted, click the selection with the secondary mouse button (the right button if you're a right-handed mouser, or the left button if you're a left-handed mouser), and choose Delete from the QuickMenu.

Deletions à la keyboard

You can use any of the following keystrokes to delete text with the keyboard:

Keystroke	Deletion
←Backspace	Character to the left of the insertion point
Delete	Character or space the insertion point is on
Ctrl+Backspace	Word the insertion point is on, including the space after the word
Ctrl+Delete	From the insertion point to the end of the current line

More stuff

Don't forget the U<u>n</u>delete command from the <u>E</u>dit menu (press Ctrl+Shift+Z) or the Undo command (press Ctrl+Z) for those times when you make a boo-boo and blow away text you shouldn't have.

For more information about this command, see Chapter 4 of *WordPerfect For Windows For Dummies*.

Document Information

Gives you oodles of statistics about your document, such as the number of characters, words, lines, sentences, and paragraphs it contains as well as the average word length and number of words per sentence.

Pull-down menu

![Screenshot of a WordPerfect window showing the File pull-down menu. The title bar reads "Display word count and other information about the current document". Menu bar: File Edit View Insert Format Table Graphics Tools Window Help. The File menu shows: New... Ctrl+T, Open... Ctrl+O, Close Ctrl+F4, Save Ctrl+S, Save As... F3, Master Document, Compare Document, Document Summary..., Document Info... (highlighted), Print... Ctrl+P, Send, Exit Alt+F4. Status bar: Insert, HP LaserJet 4 Plus/4M Plus (Win), Select, November 20, 1994, 2:01PM, Pg 1 Ln 1" Pos 1.5"]

Document Summary

Lets you add lots of different kinds of information about the document, including such stuff as a descriptive filename (rather than that cryptic DOS monstrosity) and file type (such as memo or report), the author and typist's name, and the document subject.

You then can use this information later to locate the document in the Open File dialog box (see the section "Open (File)" for details).

Pull-down menu

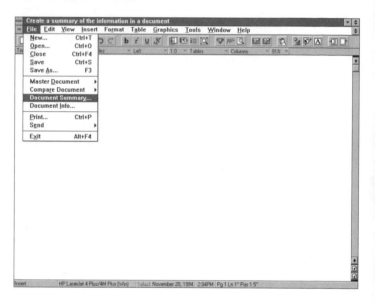

The Document Summary dialog box

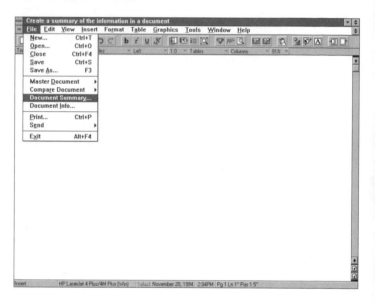

Option or Button	*Function*
Descriptive Name	Enables you to enter a long name for a file. You can list and sort files by their descriptive names in the Open File dialog box and the Save As dialog box. Choose the Setup button and then choose Descriptive Name, Filename as the Show option in the Open/Save As Setup dialog box.
Descriptive Type	Lets you enter a classification or category for a document, such as *legal brief* or *contract.* You can sort files in the Open File and Save As dialog boxes by choosing the Setup button; then choose Descriptive Type as the Sort By option in the Open/Save As Setup dialog box.
Creation Date	Indicates the date the document was created. WordPerfect for Windows automatically enters in this text box the date you create the document summary. If the date that is entered is not the date you created the document, click the Calendar button to the right of this text box and choose the correct date in the pop-up calendar. Click the single triangle to increase or decrease the month, and the double triangles to increase or decrease the year.
Revision Date	Indicates the date the document was last revised. WordPerfect for Windows automatically enters in this text box the date you create the document summary (which you cannot change).
Author	Identifies the document's author. Choose the Extract Information From Document button (from the pop-up menu attached to the Options button) to enter the name or initials of the author from the last document summary you created.
Typist	Identifies the document's typist. By using the Extract Information From Document button (from the pop-up menu attached to the Options button), you can enter the name or initials of the typist from the last document summary you created.

(continued)

Option or Button	Function
Subject	Identifies the subject of the document. Use the Extract Information From Document button (from the pop-up menu attached to the Options button) to enter the first part of the document text that follows the word or phrase identified as the Subject Search Text (RE: is used by default) in the Document Summary Preferences dialog box.
Account	Identifies the account number for the document.
Keywords	Lets you add terms you can search for later by using the QuickFinder button in the Open File dialog box.
Abstract	Lets you add a brief synopsis of the document's contents; use the Extract Information From Document button from the pop-up menu attached to the Options button to enter the first part of the document text as the document summary abstract.
Configure	Lets you choose which fields are included in the document summary.
Options	Lets you print or delete the summary, extract information according to particular fields of the summary, or save the summary in a separate file.

More stuff

You can edit a document summary from anywhere in the document by choosing the Document Summary command from the File menu. You can use the QuickFinder button in the Open File dialog box to locate documents quickly by searching their summary information.

For more information about this command, see Chapter 20 of *WordPerfect For Windows For Dummies.*

Double Indent

Indents the current paragraph one tab stop on both the left and right sides, without making you go through the trouble of changing the left and right margins.

Pull-down menu

Indent the current paragraph equally from both margins - Ctrl+Shift+F7

File   Edit   View   Insert   **Format**   Table   Graphics   Tools   Window   Help

Times New Roman   12 pt   Styl

Font...	F9
Line	
Paragraph	
Page	
Document	
Columns	
Make It Fit Expert...	
Drop Cap Ctrl+Shift+C	
Header/Footer...	
Watermark...	
Margins... Ctrl+F8	
Justification	
Typesetting	
Envelope...	
Labels...	
QuickFormat...	
Styles... Alt+F8	

Format...
Border/Fill...

Indent   F7
Hanging Indent   Ctrl+F7
Double Indent Ctrl+Shift+F7
Back Tab

Insert   HP LaserJet 4 Plus/4M Plus (Win)   Select   November 20, 1994   2:05PM   Pg 1 Ln 1" Pos 1.5"

For keyboard kronies

$\boxed{Ctrl}$ + $\boxed{Shift}$ + $\boxed{F7}$

Using double indent

The Double-Indent feature lets you use a single command to indent a paragraph of text on both sides. (For this reason, it is also known as a left-right indent.) Before you use this command, you must position the insertion point at the beginning of the paragraph, and WordPerfect for Windows must be in Insert mode. (Make sure that Typeover has replaced Insert on the Status bar.)

More stuff

When you use Double Indent, WordPerfect for Windows puts a [Hd Left/Right Ind] secret code in the text at the insertion point's position. To return the paragraph to its original layout, open the Reveal Codes window and zap this code by selecting the code and dragging it from the window, pressing Backspace over it, or placing the cursor to the left of the code and pressing Delete.

Double Indent is only one of the incredible paragraph-alignment tricks in WordPerfect for Windows. For more options, see also the sections "Hanging Indent" and plain old "Indent."

For more information about this command, see Chapter 9 of *WordPerfect For Windows For Dummies.*

Draft View

Displays your document without the top and bottom margins and without such special stuff as headers, footers, page numbers, or footnotes that show up in the top and bottom margins.

Pull-down menu

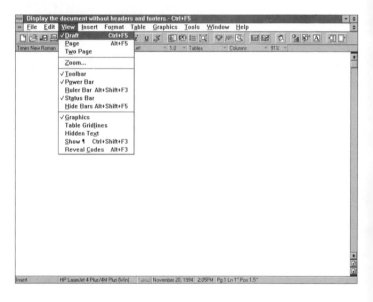

For keyboard kronies

Ctrl + F5

More stuff

Switch to draft view when you want to get the maximum amount of text on-screen for editing. Switch to page view when you want to see the relationship between the body text and the top and bottom margins or when you want to see special elements, such as headers and footers, on-screen.

See also the sections "Page View," "Two Page View," and "Zoom."

For more information about this command, see Chapter 10 of *WordPerfect For Windows For Dummies.*

Drag and Drop (Text)

Allows you mouse maniacs to move or copy selected text to a new place in the document. Just drag the selection to its new position and then drop it in place by releasing the mouse button.

Moving and copying a block with drag-and-drop

To move text with the drag-and-drop feature, select the text you want to move. You can select text by clicking it or by dragging through it. You can also select it with the cursor-movement keys. See the section "Select (Text)" for details.

After you select the text, position the mouse pointer somewhere within the selection and hold down the mouse button. Drag the mouse pointer to the new place in the document where you want the block to appear. As you drag the mouse pointer, a small rectangle appears, which indicates that the drag-and-drop process is happening. Then release the mouse button to insert the block of text in its new position in the document.

You can select the current word by double-clicking it; the sentence by triple-clicking it; and the paragraph by quadruple-clicking it.

To copy selected text rather than move it, follow the same procedure just described, but press and hold Ctrl as you drag the selected block of text.

Converts the first character of the current paragraph to a drop cap (you know, that big old capital letter that extends halfway down the left side of the paragraph's text).

Pull-down menu

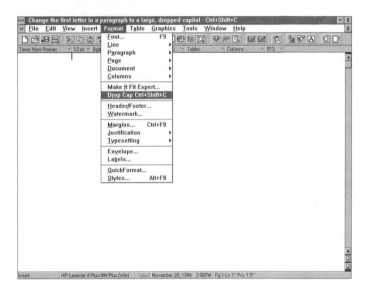

For keyboard kronies

$\boxed{Ctrl} + \boxed{Shift} + \boxed{C}$

Dropping caps with the pros

The Drop Cap feature lets you fancy-up the first paragraph of your document with a drop cap (just like you see in those highfalutin' coffee table books). To do so, simply type the text of your paragraph and then choose Drop Cap from the Format menu (or press Ctrl+Shift+C). WordPerfect then converts the very first letter in the paragraph to a drop cap.

Customized drop caps

You can use the buttons on the Drop Cap feature bar to custom-
ize the size and position of the drop cap as follows:

Option or Button	*Function*
Type	Lets you select a new drop-cap type from the pop-up palette or remove the drop cap by clicking the NO CAP button.
Size	Lets you select the number of lines you want the drop cap to take up.
Position	Lets you change the position of the drop cap in relation to the margin and the paragraph text down from the drop cap.
Font	Lets you select a new font and font attribute for the drop cap in the Drop Cap Font dialog box (which works just like the regular Font dialog box — see "Font").
Border/Fill	Lets you specify a new border and/or fill pattern for the drop cap in the Drop Cap Border dialog box (which works just like all the other Border dialog boxes in WordPerfect — see "Borders").
Options	Lets you specify other options for your drop cap, such as Make First Whole as Drop Cap (converts the entire first word to drop caps), Wrap Text around Drop Cap (the default, which you will rarely, if ever, change), Allow for Descender (lets letters in the paragraph text wrap around drop-cap letters that extend below the baseline), and Allow for Diacritic (moves the drop cap down slightly to accommodate the letter's diacritical mark — the accent mark that accompanies some of the alphabets our European cousins use).

After you finish creating and customizing your drop cap, you can
click the Close button on the Drop Cap feature bar to put it away.

More stuff

When you use the Drop Cap feature, WordPerfect for Windows puts a [Dropcap Definition] secret code at the beginning of the paragraph containing the drop cap. To remove the drop cap from the paragraph, open the Reveal Codes window and zap this code by selecting the code and dragging it from the window, pressing Backspace over it, or placing the cursor to the left of the code and pressing Delete.

Envelope

Lets you quickly address an envelope for a letter that's in the document editing window. When you use the Envelope feature, WordPerfect for Windows locates the mailing address in the letter and automatically copies it to the Mailing Addresses area of the Envelope dialog box.

Pull-down menu

The Envelope dialog box

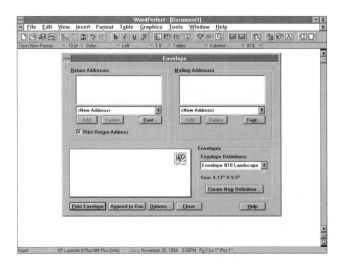

Option or Button	Function
Return Addresses	Lets you enter or edit the return address to be printed on the envelope. To select a return address you have added to the list, click the drop-down button to the right of the text box that contains <New Address> and select the address in the pop-up list. To add to this list the address you just typed, choose the Add button. To choose a new font, font size, and attributes for your address, choose Font.
Mailing Addresses	Lets you edit the mailing address that was chosen from the letter that appears in the current document window or enter a mailing address if none can be located in the current document. To choose a mailing address you have added to the New Address list, click the drop-down button to the right of the text box that contains <New Address> and make your selection from the pop-up list. To add the mailing address you typed or that WordPerfect for Windows entered in the Mailing Addresses text box, click the Add button. To choose a new font, font size, and attributes for your address, choose Font.

Option or Button	Function
Print Return Address	Prints on the envelope the address shown in the Return Addresses text box. If you're using envelopes that have your return address preprinted on them, choose this option to remove the X from its check box and make sure that no return address is printed.
Envelope Definitions	Lets you choose the envelope size you want to use. The 4.12-inch-×-9.5-inch business envelope is selected by default.
Create New Definition	Lets you create a new envelope definition if WordPerfect for Windows lacks one for the envelope you're using.
Print Envelope	Prints the envelope by using the information in the Envelope dialog box.
Append to Doc	Inserts the envelope as a separate page tacked on to the end of the document in the current document window.
Options	Lets you adjust the position of the return and mailing addresses on the envelope. Also lets you choose to have the ZIP code in your mailing address printed as a POSTNET bar code on the envelope (see the "Bar Codes" section).

More stuff

When you choose the Append to Doc button, which tacks the envelope to a new page at the bottom of your document, WordPerfect for Windows inserts a bunch of secret codes at the top of that page for formatting your new envelope. These codes include [Lft Mar], [Rgt Mar], [Top Mar], [Bot Mar], [Just], [Paper Sz/Typ], [VAdv], and [Bar Code].

For more information about this command, see Chapter 19 of *WordPerfect For Windows For Dummies.*

Exit WordPerfect

Quits WordPerfect for Windows and returns you to wherever you started the program (to either the Windows Program Manager or the File Manager).

Pull-down menu

For keyboard kronies

Alt + **F4**

More stuff

When you choose the Exit command from the File menu and have documents open that contain edits you have not saved, a message dialog box appears for each unsaved document and asks whether you want to save the changes. To save the document, choose Yes. To abandon the changes, choose No. (First be sure that you really, really don't want the information.)

Feature Bars

These bars appear at the top of the program window when you begin performing a particular task in WordPerfect for Windows (such as creating a comment or merging a data file and a form file). Each feature bar contains a series of buttons that either you keyboard kronies or you mouse maniacs can use to do things related to the task at hand.

QuickMenus

Click the feature bar with the secondary mouse button (the right button if you're a right-handed mouser, or the left button if you're a left-handed mouser) to display a list of all the feature bars included in WordPerfect for Windows. Then, to display a new feature bar, type the mnemonic key (the underlined letter) in the feature-bar name or click the feature-bar name in the list. Feature-bar names that appear dimmed in the list cannot currently be displayed.

Working the bars (feature bars, that is)

To use the mouse to select a button on a feature bar, simply click the button with the primary mouse button.

To select a feature-bar button with the keyboard, press Alt+Shift+*the button's hot key* (the underlined letter). To choose Close and close the displayed feature bar, for example, you press Alt+Shift+C.

More stuff

To find out what a particular button on a feature bar does, position the mouse pointer on the button and WordPerfect for Windows displays its function on the program window's title bar.

For more information about this command, see Chapter 10 of *WordPerfect For Windows For Dummies.*

Find and Replace

Lets you quickly locate certain text or secret codes in a document. If you use the Replace command, you can have WordPerfect for Windows replace the search text with other text, either on a case-by-case basis or globally throughout the entire document.

Pull-down menu

For keyboard kronies

To search for text or codes or search and replace them, press

[F2]

To find the next occurrence of the search text, press

[Shift] + [F2]

The Find and Replace dialog box

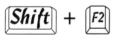

Menu/Option/Button	Function
T̲ype	Lets you choose between searching and replacing Te̲xt (the default), W̲ord Forms, or S̲pecific Codes. If you choose Word Forms, you can look for variations of the search text such as *surfed* and *surfing* when you enter **surf** as the search text; if you choose S̲pecific Codes, you can then select the secret code and enter the setting you want to search for, such as Bottom Margin 1.5", and the setting you want to replace it with, such as Bottom Margin 2".
M̲atch	Lets you search for whole words only, specify an exact case match, search for text in a particular font or attribute, or search for secret codes.
Re̲place	Lets you replace text without regard to format, text in a particular font or attribute, or certain secret codes.
D̲irection	Lets you choose between a forward or backward search-and-replace operation.
Actio̲n	Lets you specify which type of action WordPerfect should take when it finds the search text in your document. The choices include: S̲elect Match (the default), Position B̲efore (puts insertion point right in front of the first character in the search text), Position A̲fter (puts insertion point right after the last character in the search text), or E̲xtend Selection (extends the current text selection up to and including the search text).

Menu/Option/Button	Function
Options	Lets you choose from among the following: starting the search-and-replace operation at the beginning of the document, continuing the operation from the beginning of the document as soon as the program reaches the end, limiting the search to the current selection, including header and footer text in the search-and-replace operation (the default), and limiting the replacements to a specific number of times Find locates the next occurrence of the search text or codes in the document.
Replace	Replaces with the replacement text or codes the search text or codes currently located in the document.
Replace All	Replaces with the replacement text or codes all occurrences of the search text or codes in the document.

More stuff

If you ever mess up and replace a bunch of text or secret codes with the wrong stuff, immediately close the Find and Replace dialog box before you do anything else to the document. Then choose the Undo command from the Edit menu or press Ctrl+Z to put the text back to the way it was.

For more information about this command, see Chapter 5 of *WordPerfect For Windows For Dummies*.

Flush Right

Aligns a short line of text flush with the right margin.

Pull-down menu

[Screen showing WordPerfect window with "Right justify a line of text - Alt+F7" title bar. Menu bar: File Edit View Insert Format Table Graphics Tools Window Help. The Format menu is open showing: Font... F9, Line (submenu open), Paragraph, Page, Document, Columns, Make It Fit Expert..., Drop Cap Ctrl+Shift+C, Header/Footer..., Watermark..., Margins... Ctrl+F8, Justification, Typesetting, Envelope..., Labels..., QuickFormat..., Styles... Alt+F8. The Line submenu shows: Tab Set..., Height..., Spacing..., Numbering..., Hyphenation..., Center Shift+F7, Flush Right Alt+F7, Other Codes...]

For keyboard kronies

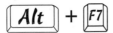

QuickMenus

Position the insertion point in front of the first character of the line to be flush right. Then click the secondary mouse button (the right button if you're a right-handed mouser, or the left button if you're a left-handed mouser) and choose Flush Right from the QuickMenu.

Flush right away

Position the insertion point at the beginning of the single line of
text you want aligned with the right margin. (The line must be terminated with a hard return.) Then press Alt+F7.

To align a new line of text with the right margin, press Alt+F7,
type the text, and press Enter. The insertion point returns to left
margin as soon as you press Enter.

To right-align several short lines of text at one time, select the
lines and press Alt+F7.

More stuff

When you use Flush Right to right-align a single line of text,
WordPerfect for Windows inserts a [Hd Flush Right] code at
the beginning of the line. When you select several short lines in a
row and use Flush Right to right-align them, WordPerfect for
Windows encloses the text in a pair of [Just> and <Just] codes
that turn right justification on and off. To return to normal left
justification at any time, simply get rid of the [Hd Flush
Right] secret code or either the [Just> or <Just] code in the
Reveal Codes window.

 You can also right-align text by changing the justification of the
document from the normal left justification to right justification.
For more information about this method, see the "Justification"
section.

For more information about this command, see Chapter 9 of
WordPerfect For Windows For Dummies.

Font

Lets you choose a new font, font size, text color, appearance, or
relative size attribute.

Pull-down menu

For keyboard kronies

QuickMenus

Click the text selection with the secondary mouse button (the right button if you're a right-handed mouser, or the left button if you're a left-handed mouser) and choose Font from the QuickMenu.

The Font dialog box

```
Indent the current paragraph equally from both margins - Ctrl+Shift+F7
File  Edit  View  Insert  Format  Table  Graphics  Tools  Window  Help
                         Font...            F9
                         Line              ▶
Times New Roman  ▼ 12 pt ▼ Sty   Paragraph          Format...                    00% ▼
                         Page              Border/Fill...
                         Document
                         Columns           Indent                   F7
                                           Hanging Indent        Ctrl+F7
                         Make It Fit Expert...  Double Indent Ctrl+Shift+F7
                         Drop Cap Ctrl+Shift+C  Back Tab

                         Header/Footer...
                         Watermark...

                         Margins...    Ctrl+F8
                         Justification      ▶
                         Typesetting        ▶

                         Envelope...
                         Labels...

                         QuickFormat...
                         Styles...     Alt+F8

Insert    Apple LaserWriter II NTX (Win)   Select  September 11, 1994  2:21PM  Pg 1 Ln 1" Pos 1"
```

WordPerfect for Windows lets you change the text font, font size, appearance, position, relative size, and color of new text all in one operation by using the Font dialog box. Before changing a font or its attributes, be sure to position the insertion point at the beginning of the text where the change is to take place.

 If you want to apply the font or font attribute to only a portion of the existing text (such as a heading), first select the text (see the "Select Text" section) and then choose your options in the Font dialog box.

Option or Button	Function
Font Face	Lets you choose a new font from the list.
Font Size	Lets you choose from the scroll window a new point size for the font. If you're using a laser printer that can scale your font to create new sizes, such as an HP LaserJet III or an Apple LaserWriter, you can type the point size in the Font Size text box if the size you want to use isn't listed.

(continued)

Option or Button	*Function*
Font Style	Enables you to choose between Regular, Italic, Bold, and Bold Italic for the font you have selected in the Selection window.
Appearance	Provides multiple appearance options for the font you have chosen, including Bold, Underline, Double Underline, Italic, Outline, Shadow, Small Cap, Redline, and Strikeout and Hidden.
Position	Lets you choose among Normal, Superscript, and Subscript as the vertical position of the font you have selected.
Relative Size	Enables you to choose a new size for your font (Fine, Small, Normal, Large, Very Large, and Extra Large), which is based entirely on a set percentage of the size of the initial font. Large is 120 percent bigger than Normal, for example. If the initial font for your printer is 10-point Courier, choosing Large gives you 12-point Courier because this size is 120 percent of the 10-point initial font.
Underline Options	By default, when you're underlining in WordPerfect for Windows, the program underlines the spaces between words. To remove underlining from the spaces, choose Spaces to remove the X from its check box. To add underlining between tabs, choose Tabs to put an X in its check box.
Color Options	Lets you specify a new color or shading for the font you have selected. To choose a new color, click the Color button and then choose the color from the pop-up color palette. To choose a new shading for the color, choose Shading and enter a new percentage in the text box. To define a custom color for the color palette, choose the Palette button and then define the new color in the Define Color Printing Palette dialog box.

Option or Button	**Function**
Font Map	Click this button if you want to change the fonts that are automatically selected when you choose a new Relative Size option. (See "Relative Size" in this table.)
Initial Font	Click this button if you want to change the font face, size, and style that are automatically selected for every new document you create for the current printer.

More stuff

The new font face, size, style, and attributes you choose stay in effect from the insertion point's position at the time of the change until you turn them off. To turn off a font change, you must choose the original font in the Font dialog box. To turn off a size change, you must select the original size in the Font dialog box.

To turn off a color change, you must select the original color (usually black) in the Color Options area of the Font dialog box. To turn off appearance changes, open the Font dialog box and deselect all the Appearance options. To turn off a relative size change, select the Normal setting for the Relative Size option in the Font dialog box. You can also turn off such appearance attributes as bold, italics, and underlining by choosing that attribute again. Either press Ctrl+B, Ctrl+I, or Ctrl+U or click **b**, *i*, or u on the WordPerfect 6.1 for Windows toolbar.

Keep in mind that if you select your text (see the "Select (Text)" section for details) and then make any of the changes offered in the Font dialog box, WordPerfect for Windows automatically turns off these attributes at the end of the selection. This way, you don't have to remember to do it yourself.

For more information about this command, see Chapter 8 of *WordPerfect For Windows For Dummies.*

Footnotes and Endnotes

Lets you add footnotes, which appear throughout the text at the bottom of every page, or endnotes, which are grouped together at the end of the document. WordPerfect for Windows automatically numbers both types of notes so that you don't have to drive yourself crazy renumbering the darn things by hand when you have to add a note or take one out.

Pull-down menus

When you're working with footnotes, choose

```
Create a new footnote
File  Edit  View  Insert  Format  Table  Graphics  Tools  Window  Help
                  Bullets & Numbers...
Times New Roman   Character...      Ctrl+W          1.0    Tables        Columns        91%
                  Abbreviations...
                  Date                ▶
                  Other               ▶
                  Footnote            ▶      Create
                  Endnote                    Edit...
                                             New Number...
                  Comment                    Options...
                  Sound...
                  Bookmark...
                  Spreadsheet/Database ▶
                  File...
                  Object...
                  Acquire Image...
                  Select Image Source...
                  Page Break    Ctrl+Enter
```

```
Insert          HP LaserJet 4 Plus/4M Plus (Win)    Select  November 20, 1994  2:10PM  Pg 1 Ln 1" Pos 1.5"
```

When you're working with endnotes, choose

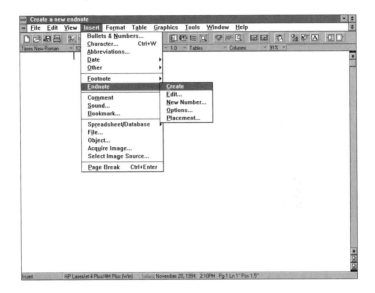

Creating a footnote or endnote

To create a footnote or an endnote in the text of your document, follow these steps:

1. Position the insertion point in the text where you want the footnote or endnote reference number to appear.

2. Choose Footnote or Endnote from the Insert menu and then choose Create. WordPerfect for Windows inserts the number of the footnote or endnote in the document and positions the insertion point at the bottom of the page (for footnotes) or the end of the document (for endnotes). At the same time, WordPerfect for Windows displays the Footnote/Endnote feature bar at the top of the page and below the Power bar.

3. Type the text of the footnote or endnote and then click the Close button on the Footnote/Endnote feature bar. When you're entering the text for your note, you can use the WordPerfect for Windows pull-down menus to select the editing and formatting commands you need in order to edit the text, including the Speller and Thesaurus.

To edit the text in a footnote or endnote, choose the Footnote or Endnote command from the Insert menu or in the Notes dialog box. Select Edit and enter the number in the Edit Footnote or Edit Endnote dialog box of the footnote or endnote to which you want to make changes. The program then positions the insertion point at the beginning of the note text so that you can make your editing changes. When you're finished editing, choose the Close button on the Footnote/Endnote feature bar.

If you're in page view (see the "Page View" section for details), you can edit the text of a footnote directly at the bottom of the page by clicking the insertion point wherever you want the edits and then begin editing. If you need to change the numbering, however, you need to edit the note as outlined in the preceding set of steps.

Changing the footnote or endnote numbering

WordPerfect for Windows automatically numbers your footnotes and endnotes and starts with the number 1. You can restart the numbering of your footnotes or endnotes at a particular place in the document (at a section break, for example) if you want. Just position the insertion point in front of the first footnote or endnote number in the text to be renumbered. (To renumber all the footnotes or endnotes in your document, move the insertion point to the beginning of the document.) Then choose Footnote or Endnote from the Insert menu and choose New Number to open the Footnote Number or Endnote Number dialog box.

To increase the note number by one, choose the OK button in the Footnote Number or Endnote Number dialog box with the Increase radio button selected (as it is by default). To decrease the note number by one, choose the Decrease radio button instead and then choose OK. To enter a nonconsecutive number, choose New Number and enter the number in its text box before you choose OK.

More stuff

When you create a footnote or endnote in the document, its reference number appears in document text and a [Footnote] or [Endnote] secret code is inserted in the Reveal Codes window. To get rid of a bogus footnote or endnote, you can simply press Backspace over this reference number in the text. (You don't have to take the time to open the Reveal Codes window and kick out the [Footnote] or [Endnote] secret codes.) WordPerfect for Windows then removes the reference number along with the footnote or endnote text.

For more information about this command, see Chapter 26 of
WordPerfect For Windows For Dummies.

Go To

Moves the insertion point to a specific place in the document,
such as its last position in the text or the top of a particular page.

Pull-down menu

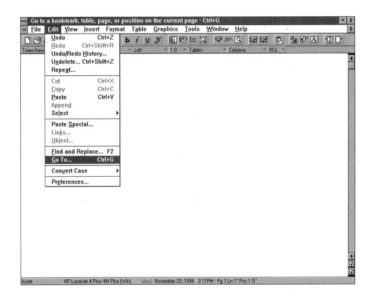

For keyboard kronies

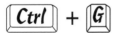

Ctrl + **G**

Go to it

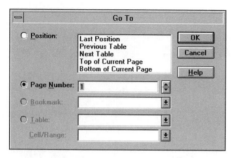

 You can choose to move the insertion point to its last known position, to the top or bottom of the current page, or to a particular page number or bookmark. (See the "Bookmark" section for information about creating bookmarks.)

To move the insertion point to a particular position, choose Go To from the Edit menu. Choose the Position radio button in the Go To dialog box and then select the specific position in the list box (Last Position, Previous Table, Next Table, Reselect Last Selection, Top of Current Page, or Bottom of Current Page).

To move the insertion point to the beginning of a particular page, choose the Page Number radio button and then enter or select the page number in its text box.

To move the insertion point to a particular bookmark, choose the Bookmark radio button. Then type the name of the bookmark in its text box or select the bookmark's name in the drop-down list.

More stuff

 If you're working with a WordPerfect for Windows table, you can move to other tables by selecting the Table radio button or by using the Previous Table or Next Table Position options. You can move to particular cells within a table by selecting the Cell/Range radio button. See the "Tables" section for information about creating tables and to find out about cells.

Graphics (Boxes)

Lets you dress up a document with clip art, charts, graphs, and scanned photographs, and with special elements, such as sidebar text and equations.

Pull-down menu

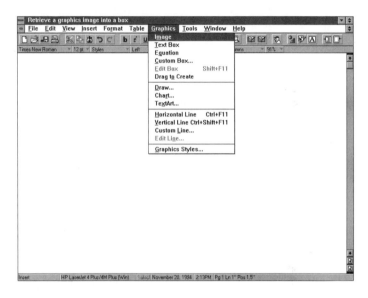

For mouse maniacs

Click ⬦ on the WordPerfect 6.1 for Windows toolbar.

QuickMenus

To display the Graphics QuickMenu, click a graphics box with the secondary mouse button (the right button if you're a right-handed mouser, or the left button if you're a left-handed mouser) to both select the box and display the menu. The Graphics QuickMenu contains lots of useful commands that let you do neat things, such as add captions, edit selected graphics, and change borders and fill patterns in the graphics box. It also lets you change the way text wraps in relation to the graphics box.

Retrieving an image

To retrieve into your document a piece of clip art or a scanned image that's saved in a disk file, position the insertion point at the place in the document where you want the image to appear. Choose Image from the Graphics menu and enter the filename in the Insert Image dialog box. Then choose OK or press Enter.

WordPerfect for Windows puts the image in a figure box that's attached to the current paragraph. At the same time, the program displays the graphics box feature bar. This image still is selected (indicated by the sizing handles — those little, black squares — that appear around the borders of the graphics box).

Little boxes

When you retrieve an image into your document, as outlined in the preceding section, WordPerfect for Windows puts the graphics file in a *figure box*. In addition to a figure box, WordPerfect for Windows offers a host of other box styles from which you can choose, each of which offers a slightly different option.

To choose another type of graphics box for the image you have added, choose Style on the graphics box feature bar while the figure box is still selected (while those little sizing jobbers are visible).

WordPerfect for Windows then opens a Box Style dialog box, in which you can choose from the following styles:

Style	*Function*
Image	The default that puts no border around the box.
Text	Puts a heavy line at the top and bottom of the graphics box. This type of graphics box appears when you choose the Text command from the Graphics menu to create a sidebar that contains a table or some text.
Equation	Does not use any type of borders. You get this type of graphics box if you're smart enough to set an equation by using the Equation command from the Graphics menu and then use (gulp!) the WordPerfect for Windows Equation Editor.

Style	*Function*
Figure	The default that puts a single-line border around the box.
User	Puts no border around the graphics box (just like the Image style).
Button	Puts the image in a graphics box that resembles a sculptured button like the one you would see on the Power bar. This style is fine if your image or text is supposed to appear as though it were inside a button (but it might not be so appropriate if the image is of your boss — he might think that you're implying that he's some sort of buttonhead!).
Watermark	Puts the image in a graphics box with no borders and makes it ghostlike (light gray) so that you can read regular text on top of it. (This style is perfect for Halloween.)
Inline Equation	Puts the image without any borders inside a paragraph, as though it were text (big text, unless you resize the graphic image to make it tiny). This graphics box style was created to make it possible for egghead mathematicians and scientists, who write papers about Diderhoff's Theorem and the possible location of the Mars probe, to include fancy (and inscrutable) equations in the middle of text.

If the graphics box feature bar is no longer displayed on-screen, you can redisplay it by clicking the graphics box with the secondary mouse button and choosing Feature Bar from the QuickMenu. Notice that many times you don't have to redisplay the feature bar because the graphics box QuickMenu provides you with commands that are comparable to the feature bar's buttons.

What a Drag to Create

WordPerfect 6.1 introduces a new feature called Drag to Create that enables you to precisely position and size a graphic before you select the image. To use this option to bring in a graphic image, follow these steps:

1. Choose Drag to Create from the Graphics pull-down menu (this puts a check mark before this command, meaning that it stays in effect until you select the command again).

2. Choose Image from the Graphics menu.

3. Position the hand-holding-a-rectangle pointer in the place in the text where the graphic image is to appear and then drag to size its graphics box. When you have the bounding rectangle the size and shape you want, release the mouse button.

4. Choose the graphics file that contains the picture you want to appear in your graphics box in the Insert Image dialog box, and then click OK or press Enter.

When you click the OK button, WordPerfect fills the graphics box you created with the Drag to Create command with the image in the graphics file you just selected.

Moving and sizing graphics boxes

After you have your graphics box in the document, you may find that you want to move the box around or make it bigger or smaller. If you're a mouse maniac, WordPerfect for Windows makes this process a snap. To move the box, just select it and drag it to its new position in the document. To resize the box, click it to make the sizing handles appear. Pick a sizing handle and begin dragging it until the box is the size and shape you want. Then release the mouse button.

This is one area in which mouse users have it all over keyboard users. If you want to move or resize a graphics box with the keyboard, you have to open the Box Position dialog box by choosing Position on the graphics box feature bar (or by choosing Position from the graphics box QuickMenu). Then you must enter the precise horizontal and vertical measurements for the graphics box in the Horizontal and Vertical text boxes, located under Position Box. (Believe me, it's much more fun to just drag the sucker around with the mouse!)

More stuff

To get rid of a graphics box, click the box to select it and press Delete to zap it out of existence.

You can play around with a graphics image inside its graphics box and move it, rotate it around, or change its size. To do so, select the graphics box and choose Tools if the graphics box feature bar is displayed (or choose Image Tools from the graphics box QuickMenu). The Tools palette is then displayed next to the graphics box. To see what each tool does, position the mouse pointer on the tool and read the description that appears on the title bar of the WordPerfect for Windows program window.

Graphics (Lines)

Lets you liven up your document with vertical or horizontal lines (also known in the design world as *rules*).

Pull-down menu

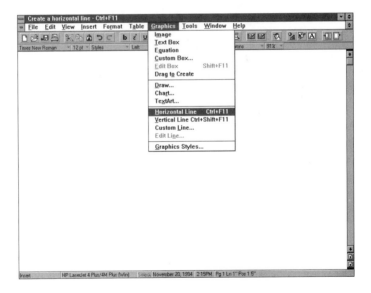

For keyboard kronies

To create a horizontal line, press

To create a vertical line, press

Toeing the line . . .

WordPerfect for Windows makes it a snap to add a horizontal or vertical line to your document. When you create a horizontal line, the length of the line is as long as the left and right document or column margins will allow. When you create a vertical line, the line is as long as the current top and bottom margins will allow (and is flush with the left margin of the document or column you're working on).

To move the graphics line, click it, drag it to its new position, and release the mouse button. To change the length of the line, drag one of the sizing handles located at each end of the line. To change the thickness of the line, drag one of the sizing handles located on the top or bottom of the midpoint of the line.

The Edit Graphics Line dialog box

If you need greater precision when you position or size the graphics line (if you're a klutz with the mouse, in other words) or you want to change the line's style or color, you must open the Edit Graphics Line dialog box. You can either double-click the graphics line to open the dialog box or choose Edit Line from the Graphics pull-down menu. After changing all the settings that have to be changed, choose OK to close the dialog box and update the settings of the graphics lines in your document.

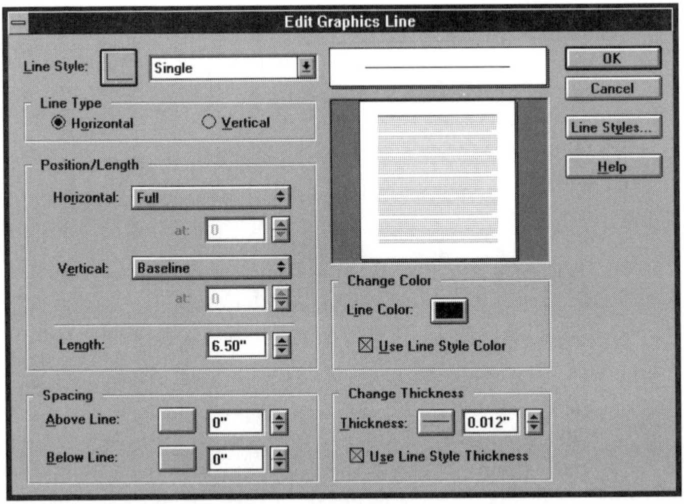

Edit Graphics Line

Line Style: [ ] Single

Line Type
- ⦿ Horizontal   ○ Vertical

Position/Length

Horizontal: Full

at: 0

Vertical: Baseline

at: 0

Length: 6.50"

Spacing

Above Line: [ ] 0"

Below Line: [ ] 0"

Change Color

Line Color: ■

☒ Use Line Style Color

Change Thickness

Thickness: 0.012"

☒ Use Line Style Thickness

OK
Cancel
Line Styles...
Help

Option or Button	Function
Line Style	Lets you choose a new line style for the graphics line. Single is the default.
Line Type	Lets you choose between a Horizontal and Vertical graphics line.
Position/Length	Lets you define the horizontal or vertical positioning of the line or specify a new length. The Horizontal option defines how the line is positioned in relation to the left and right margins. If your line is horizontal, you can choose Set, Left, Right, Centered, or Full (the default). If your line is vertical, you can choose Set, Left (the default), Right, Centered, or Column Aligned. For either type of line, use Set to specify the distance between the line and the left edge of the page.

(continued)

Option or Button	Function
	The Vertical option defines the way the line is positioned in relation to the top and bottom margins. If your line is horizontal, you can choose between Set and Baseline (the default). If your line is vertical, you can choose Set, Top, Bottom, Centered, or Full (the default). For either type of line, use Set to specify the distance between the line and the top edge of the page. The Length option lets you specify the length of either type of line. This option excludes horizontal lines whose horizontal position is Full or vertical lines whose vertical position is Full.
Spacing	Lets you specify the amount of space above and below a horizontal graphics line or between the margin and a left- or right-aligned vertical graphics line.
Change Color	Lets you specify a new color for the line.
Change Thickness	Lets you specify the thickness of the graphics line.
Line Styles	Lets you choose a new line style by name (rather than from a palette — see "Line Style" in this table) or create a custom style of your own.

More stuff

To get rid of an unwanted graphics line, click the line to select it (all those sizing jobbers appear) and then press Delete to zap it back to where it came from.

Hanging Indent

Sets off the first line of an indented paragraph by releasing it to the left margin.

Pull-down menus

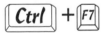

Indent all but the first line of the current paragraph one tab stop - Ctrl+F7

File   Edit   View   Insert   **Format**   Table   Graphics   Tools   Window   Help

Font...	F9
Line	▶
Paragraph	▶
Page	
Document	
Columns	

| _F_ormat... |
| _B_order/Fill... |
| _I_ndent | F7 |
| **Hanging Indent** | Ctrl+F7 |
| _D_ouble Indent Ctrl+Shift+F7 |
| Back _T_ab |

Make _I_t Fit Expert...
Drop Cap Ctrl+Shift+C

Header/Footer...
Watermark...

Margins...   Ctrl+F8
Justification   ▶
Typesetting   ▶

En_v_elope...
La_b_els...

QuickFormat...
S_t_yles...   Alt+F8

Insert   HP LaserJet 4 Plus/4M Plus (Win)   Select   November 20, 1994   2:15PM   Pg 1 Ln 1" Pos 1.5"

For keyboard kronies

$\boxed{Ctrl} + \boxed{F7}$

More stuff

Be sure that the insertion point is at the beginning of the first line of the paragraph before you choose the Hanging Indent command.

For other indenting possibilities with WordPerfect for Windows, see also the sections "Double Indent" and "Indent."

For more information about this command, see Chapter 9 of *WordPerfect For Windows For Dummies.*

Header/Footer

Adds to the document a *header,* which prints the same information at the top of each page, or a *footer,* which prints the same information at the bottom of each page.

Pull-down menu

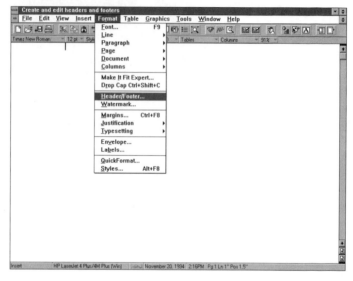

QuickMenus

Click the area at the very top or bottom of the document window when WordPerfect for Windows is in page view and choose Header/Footer from the QuickMenu.

Creating a header or footer

WordPerfect for Windows lets you create two different headers and two different footers within a document. You can have one header on all even pages and another on all odd pages, for example. To create a header or footer for the document, follow these steps:

1. Position the insertion point somewhere on the first page of the document where you want the header or footer to appear. If you want the header or footer to appear on every page of the document, make sure that your insertion point is on page one. If you don't want the header or footer to appear on the first page, make sure that your insertion point is on page two (or whichever page the header or footer appears on first).

2. Choose the Format menu and then select the Header/Footer command. This step opens the Headers/Footers dialog box.

3. To create a header, choose the Header A option. To create a footer, choose the Footer A option. (You have to fool with the Header B or Footer B options only when you add a second header or footer to a document.)

4. Choose Create to position the insertion point at either the top or bottom of the page. This step also displays the Header/Footer feature bar.

5. Type the text for your header or footer.

6. Format the header or footer text with any of the WordPerfect for Windows formatting commands from the pull-down menus or from the buttons on the Header/Footer feature bar.

7. To add a page number to your header or footer, choose Number on the Header/Footer feature bar. Then choose Page Number in the drop-down list.

8. To add a graphics line to the header or footer (see the section "Graphics (Lines)"), choose Insert Line on the Header/Footer feature bar. Then define the line in the Create Graphics Line dialog box found by choosing Custom Line from the Graphics pull-down menu.

9. Normally, WordPerfect for Windows prints your header and footer on each and every page of the document. To make the header or footer appear only on even- or odd-numbered pages, choose Pages on the feature bar and then select the Even Pages or Odd Pages option in the Pages dialog box.

10. Normally, WordPerfect for Windows separates the body of the document from the header or footer text with 0.167 inch of space (12 points). If you want to increase or decrease this spacing, choose <u>D</u>istance on the Header/Footer feature bar and enter the new value in the Distance Between Text and Header or Distance Between Text and Footer text box. You can also select this new value with the up- and down-arrow buttons located to the right of this text box.

11. When you finish entering and formatting the header or footer text, choose Close on the Header/Footer feature bar. This step hides the feature bar and returns you to the normal document window.

More stuff

When you create a header or footer, WordPerfect for Windows inserts at the top of the current page a [Header] or [Footer] secret code that identifies the letter of the header or footer. This code lets you know which header or footer (A or B) is on that page.

To see your header or footer on-screen, the program must be in page view.

To discontinue a header or footer from a certain page to the end of the document, position the insertion point on that page and open the Headers/Footers dialog box. Select the radio button for the particular header or footer (A or B) and choose <u>D</u>iscontinue.

To get rid of a header or footer from the entire document, go to the top of the first page on which it occurs and open the Reveal Codes window by pressing Alt+F3. Then zap the [Header] or [Footer] secret code by dragging it out of the Reveal Codes window or by backspacing over it.

WordPerfect for Windows also lets you create a *watermark,* which is sort of like a header or footer. It prints very lightly in the background so that the text in your document can still be read. See the "Watermark" section for details.

For more information about this command, see Chapter 10 of *WordPerfect For Windows For Dummies.*

Help

Provides help in using a particular WordPerfect for Windows feature when you're valiantly trying to figure out how to get the program to do what you want.

Pull-down menu

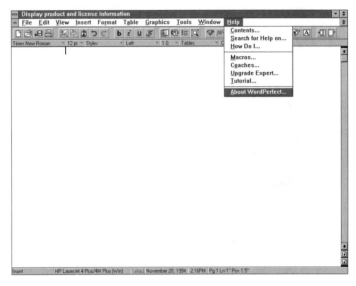

For keyboard kronies

To get general help, press

To get context-sensitive help, press

The Help menu commands

The Help menu contains the following commands:

Command	Function
Contents	Displays the WordPerfect Help window with the contents of the on-line help. To choose a topic from the Help contents, click the underlined term in the contents list.
Search for Help on	Displays the Search dialog box, in which you can locate specific help information. Type the name of the feature in the Type a word list box or choose it from the list box. Then choose Show Topics to display all the help topics related to that feature. To get help on a particular topic, choose the particular topic in the Select a topic list box. Choose Go To or press Enter.
How Do I	Displays a list of common WordPerfect for Windows tasks in the How Do I Help window. These tasks are organized in the following categories: Basics, Basic Layout, Advanced Layout, Writing Tools, Graphics/Equations, Macros, and Merge. To get help with a particular task, click the underlined term in the How Do I Help window. When you're finished, choose Close to close the How Do I Help window.
Macros	Displays the Help window with the WPWin 6.0 Online Macros Manual. To get help with a particular macro topic, click the underlined topic in this window.
Coaches	Displays an alphabetic list of topics on which WordPerfect for Windows can coach you. To have the program coach you through performing a particular task, either double-click the task or click it and choose OK or press Enter. See the "Coaches" section for more details.

Command	*Function*
Upgrade Expert	Gives specific information about how commands in WordPerfect 6.1 for Windows differ from commands in earlier DOS versions (like 5.1 and 6.0) or other Windows word processors, such as (you guessed it) Microsoft Word for Windows.
Tutorial	Starts an on-line tutorial divided into four lessons that teach you the basics of using WordPerfect for Windows. To begin a particular lesson, click the lesson to choose its radio button.
About WordPerfect	Displays the About WordPerfect dialog box, which contains a list of boring statistics about WordPerfect for Windows, such as your license number, the program's release date, and the amount of memory resources (virtual and real) that are available to your computer. The program also lets you edit the license number if someone (certainly not you) has entered it incorrectly while installing the program.

More stuff

To receive help in using a particular menu command or dialog box option as you're trying to use the darn things, highlight the command or open the dialog box and then press F1 (Help). WordPerfect for Windows opens a Help dialog box that contains information about the use of the command or the options in that dialog box. Some dialog boxes also have a Help button you can use in place of F1.

For more information about this command, see Chapter 2 of *WordPerfect For Windows For Dummies*.

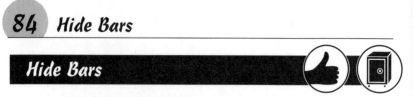

Hide Bars

Removes all the bars from the screen, including the title bar, menu bar, Power bar, toolbar, ruler bar, scroll bars, and Status bar. You see only the document text and graphics.

Pull-down menu

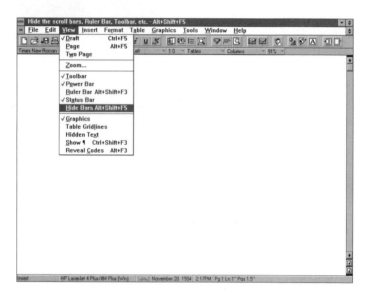

For keyboard kronies

To hide all the bars on-screen, press

$$\boxed{Alt} + \boxed{Shift} + \boxed{F5}$$

To redisplay all the hidden bars on-screen, press

$$\boxed{Esc}$$

or press

$$\boxed{Alt} + \boxed{V}$$

Then choose <u>H</u>ide Bars from the <u>V</u>iew pull-down menu.

Command	Function
<u>U</u>pgrade Expert	Gives specific information about how commands in WordPerfect 6.1 for Windows differ from commands in earlier DOS versions (like 5.1 and 6.0) or other Windows word processors, such as (you guessed it) Microsoft Word for Windows.
<u>T</u>utorial	Starts an on-line tutorial divided into four lessons that teach you the basics of using WordPerfect for Windows. To begin a particular lesson, click the lesson to choose its radio button.
<u>A</u>bout WordPerfect	Displays the About WordPerfect dialog box, which contains a list of boring statistics about WordPerfect for Windows, such as your license number, the program's release date, and the amount of memory resources (virtual and real) that are available to your computer. The program also lets you edit the license number if someone (certainly not you) has entered it incorrectly while installing the program.

More stuff

To receive help in using a particular menu command or dialog box option as you're trying to use the darn things, highlight the command or open the dialog box and then press F1 (Help). WordPerfect for Windows opens a Help dialog box that contains information about the use of the command or the options in that dialog box. Some dialog boxes also have a Help button you can use in place of F1.

For more information about this command, see Chapter 2 of *WordPerfect For Windows For Dummies*.

Hide Bars

Removes all the bars from the screen, including the title bar, menu bar, Power bar, toolbar, ruler bar, scroll bars, and Status bar. You see only the document text and graphics.

Pull-down menu

For keyboard kronies

To hide all the bars on-screen, press

 Alt + **Shift** + **F5**

To redisplay all the hidden bars on-screen, press

Esc

or press

Alt + **V**

Then choose Hide Bars from the View pull-down menu.

More stuff

When you choose this command, WordPerfect for Windows displays the Hide Bars Information dialog box. This box lets you know that you're about to hide all the bars in the WordPerfect for Windows program and document windows (including the all-important menu bar). The box also tells you how to bring the bars back. To get rid of the bars, choose OK or press Enter. If you don't want to be bothered with the display of this dialog box, choose the Disable This Message Permanently option to put an X in its check box.

In page view, what you see is more or less what you get when you print the document.

Hypertext

Lets you jump to a bookmark elsewhere in the same or even a different document (see the "Bookmark" section) or run a favorite macro (see the "Macros" section).

Pull-down menu

[Screenshot of WordPerfect window titled "Turn on the Hypertext Feature Bar" showing menu bar: File Edit View Insert Format Table Graphics Tools Window Help. The Tools menu is open showing: Spell Check... Ctrl+F1, Thesaurus... Alt+F1, Grammatik... Alt+Shift+F1, QuickCorrect... Ctrl+Shift+F1, Language..., Macro ▸, Template Macro ▸, Merge... Shift+F9, Sort... Alt+F9, Outline, Hypertext (highlighted), List, Index, Cross-Reference, Table of Contents, Table of Authorities, Generate... Ctrl+F9. Status bar shows: HP LaserJet 4 Plus/4M Plus (Win) Select November 20, 1994 2:17PM Pg 1 Ln 1" Pos 1.5"]

The Hypertext feature bar

Button	Function
P<u>e</u>rform	Jumps to the bookmark associated with the hypertext link (or runs the macro you have associated with the link).
<u>B</u>ack	Takes you from the bookmark where the cursor lies to the hypertext link you just came from.
<u>N</u>ext	Takes you to the next hypertext link in the document.
<u>P</u>revious	Takes you to the preceding hypertext link in the document.
Crea<u>t</u>e	Lets you create a link to a particular bookmark that exists in this or another document or to a macro you want to run; when you create a link to a bookmark or macro, you can also indicate whether the text with the hypertext link should appear as underlined text in another color or in a button that is sculptured.
<u>E</u>dit	Lets you edit a particular hypertext link.
<u>D</u>elete	Lets you get rid of a particular hypertext link.
De<u>a</u>ctivate	Lets you activate the Hypertext feature in your document so that you jump to and return from a linked bookmark or run a linked macro.
<u>S</u>tyle	Lets you monkey with the style used to display a hypertext link in a document.
<u>C</u>lose	Hides the Hypertext feature bar.

More stuff

Before you can create a hypertext link, you must create the bookmarks (see the "Bookmark" section) or macros (see the "Macros" section) to which you want to link. Then you must select the text you want to designate as the hypertext link. This text activates the link to the bookmark or macro.

After you create a hypertext link, you can jump to the linked bookmark or run the macro by clicking the (hyper)text button or choosing Perform on the Hypertext feature bar.

To return to the hypertext after you have jumped to a bookmark either in the current or a different document, choose Back on the Hypertext feature bar.

If you click a hypertext link and nothing happens (no jump, no macro, no nothing), the Hypertext feature has been deactivated. To reactivate it, open the Hypertext feature bar and click Activate (which then turns into Deactivate).

For more information about this command, see Chapter 26 of *WordPerfect For Windows For Dummies.*

Hyphenation

Automatically hyphenates words in a paragraph to reduce the raggedness of the right margin (when you're using left justification) or the white space between words in the lines (when you're using full justification).

Pull-down menu

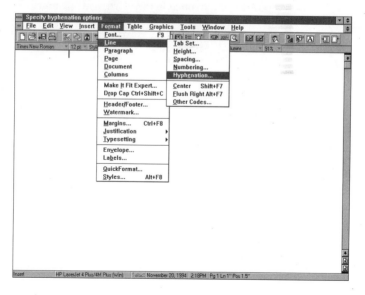

Using the Hyphenation feature

To have WordPerfect for Windows automatically hyphenate the words in your document according to the program's dictionary, follow these steps:

1. Position the insertion point at the place in the document where you want to turn hyphenation on. To hyphenate the entire document, press Ctrl+Home, which moves the insertion point to the beginning of the document.

2. Choose Line from the Format menu and then choose Hyphenation.

3. Select Hyphenation On to put an X in its check box and then click OK or press Enter. WordPerfect for Windows inserts the [Hyph] code in the document and from that point on hyphenates the document as required by the hyphenation zone.

   As you add text from the insertion point's position or scroll through the document, WordPerfect for Windows displays the Position Hyphen dialog box. This box prompts you to confirm its suggested hyphenation of the word (if that word isn't in the spelling dictionary).

4. To accept the position of the hyphen as it is displayed in the Position Hyphen dialog box, select Insert Hyphen. To reposition the hyphen in the word, use the mouse or the arrow keys to position the hyphen in the proper place and then choose Insert Hyphen. To insert a space rather than a hyphen, choose Insert Space. To insert a hyphenation soft return to break the word without inserting a space, choose Hyphenation SRt. To temporarily suspend the hyphenation (so that you can do something else, such as scroll the text or check its spelling), choose Suspend Hyphenation. To have WordPerfect for Windows wrap the entire word to the next line rather than break the word with a hyphen, space, or hyphenation soft return, choose Ignore Word.

5. To turn off hyphenation at the beginning of the paragraph that contains the insertion point, choose Line from the Format menu and then choose Hyphenation. Remove the X from the Hyphenation On check box and click OK or press Enter. From this point on, WordPerfect for Windows simply wraps around to the next line the words that extend beyond the right margin.

More stuff

WordPerfect for Windows inserts a [Hyph] secret code in the document where you turn on hyphenation. When WordPerfect for Windows prompts you to hyphenate a word and instead you choose Ignore Word, the program inserts a [Cancel Hyph] secret code in the document. This code appears in front of the word that's not hyphenated and wraps the word to the next line.

WordPerfect for Windows maintains a hot zone, made up of the left and right hyphenation zones, that determines when a word is up for hyphenation. To be a candidate for hyphenation, a word must begin within the left zone and then extend beyond the right zone. To change how often WordPerfect for Windows bugs you to hyphenate words, you can monkey around with the size of the left and right zones. To do so, open the Line Hyphenation dialog box and change the percentages in the Percent Left and Percent Right text boxes. Increasing the zone percentages hyphenates fewer words and decreasing the percentages hyphenates more words.

For more information about this command, see Chapter 9 of *WordPerfect For Windows For Dummies.*

Indent

Moves the left edge of an entire paragraph one tab stop to the right, which creates an indent that sets the paragraph off from normal text.

Pull-down menu

For keyboard kronies

QuickMenus

Position the insertion point in front of the first character in the line to be indented. Then click the secondary mouse button (the right button if you're a right-handed mouser, or the left button if you're a left-handed mouser) and choose Indent from the QuickMenu.

More stuff

When you indent a paragraph, WordPerfect for Windows inserts a [Hd Left Ind] secret code at the insertion point's position in the line. To remove an indent you insert by accident, open the Reveal Codes window and zap this [Hd Left Ind] jobber.

Also, be sure that the insertion point is at the very beginning of the paragraph before you indent it.

For information about the other types of indents that are possible with WordPerfect for Windows, see also the sections "Double Indent" and "Hanging Indent."

For more information about this command, see Chapter 9 of *WordPerfect For Windows For Dummies.*

Insert Filename

Lets you insert the document's filename (with or without its inscrutable pathname) into your document. You can use this nifty feature to add the filename to your header or footer so that you can cross-reference the printout with its disk file.

Pull-down menu

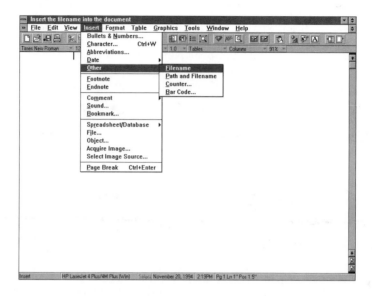

Insert the filename

To insert just the filename of your document, choose Other from the Insert pull-down menu and choose Filename from the cascading menu. To insert the filename plus its entire directory path (starting with C: or whatever the heck the drive letter is), choose Path and Filename from this cascading menu instead.

More stuff

WordPerfect for Windows inserts into the document a [Filename] secret code that produces the filename (with or without the directory path). The program automatically updates the filename if you rename the document with the Save As command from the File menu. You can even use this feature to insert the filename command before you initially save the document with a filename. The place where [Filename] exists in the document remains blank until you name and save the file. When you finally save it — presto! — the filename magically appears in the document where the [Filename] code is.

Insertion Point

Before you edit the text of your document, you have to position the insertion point in the correct place. WordPerfect for Windows restricts insertion-point movement to the existing text in a document and never lets you move it beyond the last character in a document.

Moving the insertion point with the keyboard

WordPerfect for Windows offers a variety of ways to move the insertion point with the keyboard, as shown in this table:

Keystrokes	*Where Insertion Point Moves*
←	Next character or space to the left
→	Next character or space to the right
Ctrl+←	Beginning of next word to the left
Ctrl+→	Beginning of next word to the right
Ctrl+↑	Beginning of current or preceding paragraph
Ctrl+↓	Beginning of next paragraph
Home	Left edge of current screen or beginning of current line
End	Right edge of current screen or end of current line
Ctrl+Home	Beginning of document
Ctrl+End	End of document
PgUp	Up a screenful
PgDn	Down a screenful
Alt+PgUp	Top of current page
Alt+PgDn	Top of next page
Ctrl+PgUp	One screenful to the left
Ctrl+PgDn	One screenful to the right

For mouse maniacs

If you use the mouse, you can reposition the insertion point in the document text by placing the mouse pointer on the character or space and clicking the primary mouse button.

More stuff

Don't confuse the insertion point with the mouse pointer (as easy as that is to do). The insertion point keeps your place in the document as it continues to blink. The mouse pointer enables you to select things (as well as reposition the insertion point in the text). Mostly, the mouse pointer just lies there on-screen, not doing anything useful and getting in the way until you move the mouse.

For more information about using the insertion point, see Chapter 3 of *WordPerfect For Windows For Dummies*.

Justification

Changes the way paragraphs are aligned in a document. You can choose L̲eft (which gives you a flush left but ragged right margin), R̲ight (which gives you a flush right but ragged left margin), Ce̲nter (which centers all lines between the left and right margins), F̲ull (which gives you a flush left and flush right margin), and A̲ll justification (which forces justification even in the last, short line of each paragraph so that the line is flush left and right, like all the other full lines).

Pull-down menu

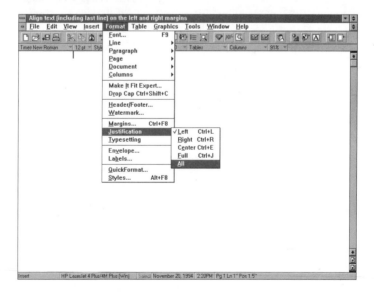

For keyboard kronies

For left justification, press

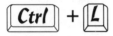 + *L*

For center justification, press

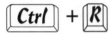 + *E*

For right justification, press

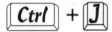 + *R*

For full justification, press

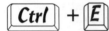 + *J*

For mouse maniacs

You can change the justification in your document with the Justification button on the Power bar. To do so, click this button (which shows Left as the justification unless you've changed it) in the Power bar and then select the desired justification in the pop-up menu (Left, Right, Center, Full, or All).

More stuff

When you change the justification in a document, WordPerfect for Windows inserts a [Just] secret code. Unlike changing the alignment with the Center or Flush Right commands, which only affect the text from the current line to the hard return ([HRt] secret code) that begins the next paragraph, changes in the justification of a document affect all text beginning with the [Just] secret code. To return the text to normal left justification, position the cursor where the text should return to normal and choose Justification from the Format menu. Then choose Left to return to normal left justification.

 For more information about this command, see Chapter 9 of *WordPerfect For Windows For Dummies.*

Keep Text Together

Keeps sections of text from being split apart on different pages of
a document. WordPerfect for Windows offers several methods for
doing so in the Keep Text Together dialog box.

Pull-down menu

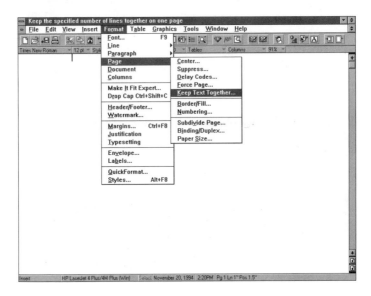

The Keep Text Together dialog box

Option or Button	Function
Widow/Orphan	Prevents the first or last line of a paragraph from being split apart across pages.
Block Protect	Keeps the block of selected text from ever being split apart on different pages.
Conditional End of Page	Keeps a specified number of lines together on a page; you enter in the text box the number of lines you want to keep together (as counted down from the insertion point's current position).

More stuff

If you want to keep a title with its first paragraph or a table of data together and you don't know the number of lines to specify, select all the text and then choose Keep selected text together on same page under Block Protect.

For more information about this command, see Chapter 10 and Chapter 16 of *WordPerfect For Windows For Dummies*.

Labels

Formats address labels so that you can use the labels to send mass mailings.

Pull-down menu

![Screenshot of WordPerfect window with Format menu open showing options including Font, Line, Paragraph, Page, Document, Columns, Make It Fit Expert, Drop Cap Ctrl+Shift+C, Header/Footer, Watermark, Margins Ctrl+F8, Justification, Typesetting, Envelope, Labels (highlighted), QuickFormat, Styles Alt+F8]

The Labels dialog box

Option or Button	Function
Display	Lets you choose which types of label definitions are displayed in the Labels list box. Choose Laser, Tractor-Fed, or Both (the default).
Labels	Lets you use the associated list box to choose by name the type of labels to use. When you choose a label in this list, the program displays the sheet size, label size, number of labels on a sheet, and the label type in the Label Details area of the dialog box.
Change	Lets you select, create, or edit a new file of label definitions for use with your printer. The file you select here appears after Label File in the Select Label File area of the dialog box (by default, this file is wp_wp_us.lab).
Select	Selects the labels highlighted in the Labels list box.
Off	Turns off labels in a document and returns you to the normal paper size and type for your printer (usually letter size).

(continued)

Option or Button	Function
Create	Lets you create a new label definition if none of the predefined labels are suitable.
Edit	Lets you modify the predefined label definition that's selected in the Labels list box.
Delete	Lets you delete the label definition selected in the Labels list box.

More stuff

When you select a label form that has multiple labels on a single physical page, WordPerfect for Windows treats each label as its own page on-screen. In other words, the Page indicator changes as you go from label to label. To begin filling in a new label, therefore, press Ctrl+Enter (which is a hard page break). To move from page to page, press Alt+PgDn or Alt+PgUp.

 To see how each individual label will look, be sure that the program is in page view rather than in draft view.

For more information about this command, see Chapter 22 of *WordPerfect For Windows For Dummies*.

Line Height

Lets you control how much blank space WordPerfect for Windows puts between each line of text on a page (something the program normally takes care of automatically).

Pull-down menu

Changing line height

To use a *fixed* (rather than flexible) line height, open the Line Height dialog box and choose the Fixed radio button. Enter the new measurement (as measured from the baseline of one line to the baseline of the next line) in the text box or select it with the up- and down-arrow buttons. Then choose OK or press Enter.

More stuff

Most of the time, you don't have to monkey around with the line height. WordPerfect for Windows automatically increases the height as necessary to accommodate the largest font you use in a line. Once in a blue moon, however, you may have a situation in which you want to increase or decrease the amount of space between certain lines of text without changing the line spacing.

When you fix the line height, the new height remains in effect for all subsequent lines in the document. If you reach a place where you want WordPerfect for Windows to determine the best line height for your text, place the insertion point at the beginning of the line. Then open the Line Height dialog box and this time choose the Auto radio button.

Line Numbering

Numbers the lines on each page of your document.

Pull-down menu

The Line Numbering dialog box

Option or Button	Function
Turn Line Numbering On	Lets you turn line numbering on and off at the current position of the insertion point. If this check box has an X in it, line numbering is turned on; if the check box is empty, line numbering is off.
Numbering Method	Lets you choose a new numbering method from the following: Number (the default), Lowercase Letter, Uppercase Letter, Lowercase Roman, or Uppercase Roman.
Starting Line Number	Lets you change the starting line (1 is the default).
First Printing Line Number	Lets you choose the first line number to be printed in the document (1 is the default).
Numbering Interval	Lets you change the interval between the numbers printed in the document (1 is the default).

Option or Button	Function
Position of Numbers	Lets you change the position of the line numbers. You can choose whether you want the distance to be measured From Left Edge of Page or from Left of Margin.
Restart Numbering on Each Page	Enables WordPerfect for Windows to restart the numbering (from the Starting Line Number) on each new page of the document.
Count Blank Lines	Lets you determine whether blank lines are counted in the line numbering. (They are, by default.)
Number all Newspaper Columns	Lets you determine whether each newspaper column on the page gets line numbers.
Font	Lets you choose new fonts, attributes, and colors for the line numbers.

More stuff

When you want to turn off line numbering, position the insertion point at the beginning of the first line that is not to be numbered. Open the Line Numbering dialog box and choose Turn Line Numbering On to remove the X from the check box. Then choose OK or press Enter.

For more information about this command, see Chapter 26 of *WordPerfect For Windows For Dummies.*

Line Spacing

Changes the line spacing of the text in your document.

Pull-down menu

Spacing out

To change line spacing, position the insertion point on the first line to be affected. Open the Line Spacing dialog box and enter the new spacing in the Spacing text box (or select the new spacing with the up- and down-arrow buttons). Then choose OK or press Enter.

More stuff

When you set the line spacing for your document, WordPerfect for Windows lets you enter values in increments that are smaller than one-half line. Keep in mind, however, that your printer may not be able to handle anything smaller than a half line. Whenever possible, WordPerfect for Windows displays the new line spacing on-screen more or less as it prints.

For more information about this command, see Chapter 9 of *WordPerfect For Windows For Dummies.*

Macros

Lets you record a series of commands that WordPerfect for Windows can play back later at a much faster rate than you can possibly do manually.

Pull-down menu

For keyboard kronies

To play a macro, press

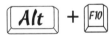

To record a new macro, press

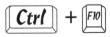

Recording macros

Recording macros in WordPerfect for Windows resembles the way you record cassette tapes or videotapes. After you turn on the macro recorder, WordPerfect for Windows records the result of each action you perform, whether you type some text or choose new format settings.

You can use the macro recorder to record several types of series. WordPerfect for Windows can record a straight series of commands, such as changing the top margin to two inches and the line spacing to double spacing. It can record a straight series of words or phrases, such as *Abercrombie, Fitch, Abercrombie and Phelps.* Or the program can record a combination of text and commands, such as entering the company name *Baggins and Bilbo, Inc.* and then centering and boldfacing this text before inserting two blank lines.

To record a macro, follow these steps:

1. Position the insertion point at a place in your document where it's safe (and possible) to execute all the WordPerfect for Windows commands you want to record in your macro.

2. Choose Macro from the Tools menu and then choose Record or simply press Ctrl+F10.

3. Enter a name for your macro in the Name text box. The name can be as long as eight characters. Alternatively, you can name a macro CTRL*x* or CTRLSFT*x,* where *x* represents a character, such as *K.* You can use any keyboard character (A through Z or 0 through 9) after CTRL or CTRLSFT to name your macro. WordPerfect for Windows then saves your macro under this filename with the .WCM extension when you finish recording the macro.

   If you're recording a quick macro (which is essentially a temporary, unnamed macro that you're using only during the current work session), leave the Name text box empty.

4. Select Record or press Enter to begin recording the macro.

   WordPerfect for Windows closes the Record Macro dialog box, changes the mouse pointer to the international "Don't" symbol (a circle with a line through it) to remind you that mouse moves don't work when you record a macro in WordPerfect for Windows 6.1 (see the "More stuff" section), and displays the Macro Record message on the Status bar to remind you that all your actions are being recorded.

If the filename you specified for the macro already exists, WordPerfect for Windows displays a message dialog box that asks whether you want to replace the existing macro. Choose Yes to replace the existing macro with the one you are about to create. Choose No if you want to save the macro under a different name.

5. Enter the text and select the commands you want to include in your macro. Make sure to select them in the sequence in which you want to record them. If you want to move the insertion point or select text, you must use the keyboard. (When you're recording a macro, you can use the mouse only to choose menu commands and make selections in dialog boxes.)

6. When you're finished choosing the WordPerfect for Windows commands and entering the text for the macro, choose Macro from the Tools menu. Then choose Record from the cascading menu (or just press Ctrl+F10 again).

WordPerfect for Windows immediately turns off the macro recorder, and the Macro Record message disappears from the Status bar.

Playing back macros

To play back a CTRL*x* or CTRLSFT*x* macro, simply press Ctrl and the letter key or press Ctrl+Shift and the letter key. To play back a macro with a regular filename, choose Macro from the Tools menu and choose Play or simply press Alt+F10. Type the macro's filename (without its .WCM extension) and press Enter or choose OK.

When you play back a macro, WordPerfect for Windows plays back each command in the sequence in which it was recorded. If your macro is not behaving as expected, you can stop the playback by pressing Esc. Because of the potential danger in playing back an untested macro, you should always make sure to save the current document before you play back a macro for the first time. Then, if the macro wreaks havoc in your document before you can shut it down with Esc, you can always close the trashed document without saving your changes and then open the version you saved before performing the macro.

Attaching your macro to the document template

When you choose Macro from the Tools menu, WordPerfect for Windows saves the new macro in its own file. To attach the new macro to the current template (see "New (Document)") for details, choose Template Macro from the Tools menu and then select its Record command. WordPerfect then displays the Record Template Macro dialog box, where you enter the new macro's name in its Name text box. By default, WordPerfect for Windows attaches the macro to whichever template is currently assigned to your document (making this macro available to any document using the same template). If you want your new macro attached to the default template (instead of the current template), click the Location button and then select the Default Template radio button in the Macro Location dialog box.

After naming your macro in the Record Template Macro dialog box, click the Record button and then record your macro as you would record one saved in its own file.

More stuff

If you're a mouse maniac, you can use the mouse as you record the macro. You can use it to choose the WordPerfect for Windows commands from the pull-down menus and in the dialog boxes you want to include. If you want to record insertion-point movements as part of the macro, however, you must abandon the mouse and switch to the insertion-point movement keys.

WordPerfect for Windows cannot record the movements of the insertion point in the text that you make by clicking the mouse or using the scroll bars. (See the "Insertion Point" section for specific keystrokes.)

For more information about this command, see Chapter 26 of *WordPerfect For Windows For Dummies.*

Make It Fit Expert

Lets you puff up or shrink the text and graphics in your document so that they fit within a set number of pages.

Pull-down menu

```
┌─ Shrink or expand document to fill page ─────────────────────────────┐
│ File  Edit  View  Insert  Format  Table  Graphics  Tools  Window  Help │
├──────────────────────────────────────────────────────────────────────┤
```

Font...	F9
Line	▶
Paragraph	▶
Page	▶
Document	▶
Columns	▶
Make It Fit Expert...
Drop Cap Ctrl+Shift+C
Header/Footer...
Watermark...
Margins...   Ctrl+F8
Justification	▶
Typesetting	▶
Envelope...
Labels...
QuickFormat...
Styles...   Alt+F8

Times New Roman   12 pt   Styl   Tables   Columns   91%

Insert   HP LaserJet 4 Plus/4M Plus (Win)   Select   November 20, 1994   2:25PM   Pg 1 Ln 1" Pos 1.5"

For mouse maniacs

Click 🔍 on the WordPerfect 6.1 for Windows toolbar to open the
Make It Fit Expert dialog box.

The Make It Fit Expert dialog box

```
┌─────────────────── Make It Fit Expert ───────────────────┐
│ ┌─Pages────────────────────────────┐   ┌───────────────┐ │
│ │ Current Number of Pages:   1     │   │  Make It Fit  │ │
│ │                                  │   └───────────────┘ │
│ │ Desired Number of Filled Pages: [1] ⬍  ┌───────────┐  │
│ └──────────────────────────────────┘   │  Cancel   │   │
│                                         └───────────┘   │
│ ┌─Items to Adjust──────────────────┐   ┌───────────┐    │
│ │ □ Left Margin    ☒ Font Size     │   │   Help    │    │
│ │ □ Right Margin   ☒ Line Spacing  │   └───────────┘    │
│ │ □ Top Margin                     │                    │
│ │ □ Bottom Margin                  │                    │
│ └──────────────────────────────────┘                    │
│                                                          │
│ When Make It Fit is finished, you may press Ctrl+Z or click │
│ the Undo button to return the document to its original state. │
└──────────────────────────────────────────────────────────┘
```

Option	Function
Desired Number of Filled Pages	Lets you specify how many pages of WordPerfect should expand or compress the document text to fit into.
Left Margin	When this option is checked, WordPerfect increases or decreases the left margin as required to make the document fit in the specified number of pages.
Right Margin	When this option is checked, WordPerfect increases or decreases the right margin as required to make the document fit in the specified number of pages.
Top Margin	When this option is checked, WordPerfect increases or decreases the top margin as required to make the document fit in the specified number of pages.
Bottom Margin	When this option is checked, WordPerfect increases or decreases the bottom margin as required to make the document fit in the specified number of pages.
Font Size	When this option is checked, WordPerfect increases or decreases the size of the fonts used in the text as required to make the document fit in the specified number of pages.
Line Spacing	When this option is checked, WordPerfect increases or decreases the line spacing used in the text as required to make the document fit in the specified number of pages.

More stuff

WordPerfect puts no secret code into your document when you use the Make It Fit Expert to expand or shrink your document. Therefore, you must resort to the Undo feature (Ctrl+Z) to restore your document to its original page count should your Make

It Fit endeavor end in disaster. You might also do yourself a favor
and use the File⇨Save As command to save the resized document
as a separate file under a new name (so that you always have access to the original) before you try printing your expanded or
compressed version.

Margins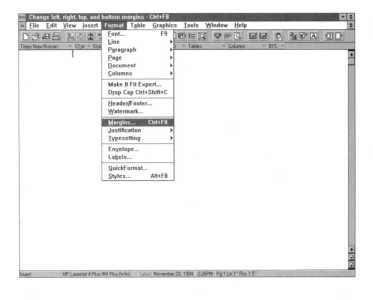

Lets you set new left, right, top, and bottom margins for your
document.

Pull-down menu

For keyboard kronies

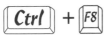

For mouse maniacs

You can change the left and right margins by dragging the left- and right-margin icons located on the ruler bar. To display the ruler bar, choose Ruler Bar from the View menu or press Alt+Shift+F3.

To display the Margins dialog box, double-click the left or right margin (or the white space between them) on the ruler bar, above the tab ruler.

QuickMenus

Click the left margin area of the document window with the secondary mouse button (the right button if you're a right-handed mouser or the left button if you're a left-handed mouser) and choose Margins from the QuickMenu.

The changing of the margins

To change margins, position the insertion point on the line on which the new left and right margins will take effect or on the page on which the new top and bottom margins will take effect. Open the Margins dialog box and select the margin text box you want to change (Left, Right, Top, or Bottom). Then enter the new margin setting or select it with the up- and down-arrow buttons located to the right of the text box.

More stuff

When you change the margin settings, WordPerfect for Windows inserts at the beginning of the current paragraph some secret codes that are specific to the margins you changed. To return to the default margin settings, open the Reveal Codes window and zap the offending [Lft Mar], [Rgt Mar], [Top Mar], or [Bot Mar] secret code.

For more information about this command, see Chapter 9 of *WordPerfect For Windows For Dummies*.

Merge

Generates "personalized" form letters and other documents that consist of canned text plus variable information. This variable information is dropped in from a data file.

Pull-down menu

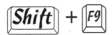

For keyboard kronies

Shift + **F9**

Creating a table data file

Before you can perform a merge, you have to create a data file and a form file. A *data file* contains the data records you want to use in the merge (such as the names and addresses of clients). A *form file* indicates where the information in each record will be merged. The easiest way to create a data file is to set it up as a table:

1. Choose M̲erge from the T̲ools menu or press Shift+F9 to open the Merge dialog box.

2. Choose P̲lace Records in a Table to put an X in its check box. Then choose D̲ata or press Enter.

3. If the current document is not empty, the Create Merge File dialog box appears with the Use File in Active Window radio button selected. To create the data file in the current document window, choose OK or press Enter. To create the data file in a new document window, choose the New Document Window radio button before you choose OK or press Enter.

4. WordPerfect for Windows then displays the Create Data File dialog box, in which you name the *fields* (pieces of information) you want to use in the new data file. For each field you want, enter a descriptive name for that field in the Name a Field text box. Press Enter or choose Add after typing each field name to add it to the Field Name List box. When you finish adding field names, choose OK or press Enter (without entering a name in the Name a Field text box), which closes the Create Data File dialog box and creates the table.

   After closing the Create Data File dialog box, WordPerfect for Windows automatically opens the Quick Data Entry dialog box.

5. Fill out the first record in the Quick Data Entry dialog box by entering information in each field listed in the Record area. After you finish entering information in a field, advance to the next field by pressing Tab or choosing Next Field. If you want to edit a previous field, press Shift+Tab or choose Previous Field. When you finish entering the information for the last field, press Enter or choose New Record. This step adds the information for the first record to the new data table and clears all the fields in the Quick Data Entry dialog box for your next record entry.

6. Repeat step 5 to continue adding records to the new data file. When you finish adding your last record, choose Close to close the Quick Data Entry dialog box.

7. WordPerfect for Windows displays an Alert dialog box that asks whether you want to save the changes to disk. Choose Yes to save the document that contains the new data file. Then enter the new filename in the Save Data File dialog box and choose OK.

   If you prefer to wait and save the document after you have a chance to check over the data table, choose No instead.

Creating a form file

After you create a data file with the data records, you have to create a form file, which indicates how and where each piece of information (*field*) from the data file is used. The form file contains both boilerplate text and field codes that say "Put this piece of information from each record right here." To create a form file, follow these steps:

1. Choose Merge from the Tools menu or press Shift+F9 to open the Merge dialog box.

2. Choose Form.

3. If the current document is not empty, the Create Merge File dialog box appears with the Use File in Active Window radio button selected. To create the data file in the current document window, choose OK or press Enter. To create the data file in a new document window, choose the New Document Window radio button before you choose OK or press Enter.

    WordPerfect for Windows then opens the Create Form File dialog box, which is where you indicate the data file you're using for the merge with the new form file.

4. Insert the filename of the data file in the Associate a Data File text box by typing the filename or by selecting it with the list-file button to the right of this text box. Then choose OK or press Enter. If you don't know which data file you will use with the form file you're creating, choose the None radio button.

    WordPerfect for Windows then closes the Create Form File dialog box and returns you to a new (or the current) document window. At the same time, the program displays the Merge feature bar.

5. Type the standard text in your form document. Insert FIELD merge codes (described in step 6) at each place in the text where you want WordPerfect for Windows to merge information from the records in the data file. Be sure to include all necessary punctuation and spaces between FIELD codes.

6. To insert a FIELD merge code in the form file, choose Insert Field on the Merge feature bar. Then select the field to use in the Field Names list box of the Insert Field Name or Number dialog box and press Enter or choose Insert. Repeat this procedure for each field you want merged from the data file.

Every time you perform this procedure, WordPerfect for Windows inserts the FIELD merge code with the name of the field you selected. If you selected the Company field, for example, you see FIELD(Company) in the text.

7. To insert the current date in the text of the form letter, choose Date in the Merge feature bar.

    WordPerfect for Windows then inserts the DATE merge code at the insertion point's current position.

8. When you're finished composing the form document by combining the canned text with the appropriate field names, save the file by using Save or Save As from the File menu (or by pressing Ctrl+S). When you name your data file, you can add an extension (such as .FRM, for form file) to differentiate this form file from other standard document files.

Merging the data and form file

After you have created your data and form files, you're ready to rock 'n' roll (well, at least to perform the merge). To perform the standard merge, follow these steps:

1. Choose Open from the File menu to open the form file you want to use in the merge.

2. Open the Merge dialog box by choosing Merge on the Merge feature bar, by choosing Merge from the Tools menu, or by pressing Shift+F9.

3. Choose Merge in the Merge dialog box to open the Perform Merge dialog box.

4. Select the form, data, and output files under Files to Merge in the Perform Merge dialog box.

    By default, you see <Current Document> in the Form File text box, the associated data file in the Data File text box, and <New Document> in the Output File text box. Change any of these settings as necessary by selecting the appropriate text box. Then enter the filename or select it with the list-file button located to the right of each text box.

5. Choose OK or press Enter to begin the merge. The program merges information from records in the data file with copies of the form file, creating a new merged form for each record used. WordPerfect for Windows keeps you informed by showing its progress on the Status bar.

More stuff

Keep in mind that you can have WordPerfect for Windows generate an envelope for each form letter you create in the merge. To
do so, choose Envelopes in the Perform Merge dialog box. Then
fill out the information in the Envelope dialog box, including using
the Field button to copy the appropriate FIELD codes from the
data file into the Mailing Addresses area of the Envelope dialog
box. WordPerfect for Windows then generates an envelope for
each record during the merge and places all the envelopes after
the form letters that are produced (see the "Envelope" section).

To create mailing labels for your form letters, you have to create
a form file that you insert into just the first label. This file uses a
label form with the appropriate FIELD codes for the associated
data file. Then you perform a merge by using this label form file
and the data file whose fields are referred to. (See the "Labels"
section for more information.)

For more information about this command, see Chapter 18 of
WordPerfect For Windows For Dummies.

New (Document)

Opens a brand-new document in another document editing window.

Pull-down menu

For keyboard kronies

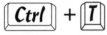

For mouse maniacs

To insert a new document using the default template, click on the WordPerfect 6.1 for Windows toolbar. To insert a new document and select another template for it, click on this toolbar.

Selecting a template for the new document

When you choose the New command on the File menu, press Ctrl+T, or click on the WordPerfect 6.1 for Windows toolbar. WordPerfect opens the New Document dialog box, where you can select the template that you want to associate with the new document that you're opening.

WordPerfect 6.1 for Windows comes with a whole bunch of premade templates that you can use for different types of documents. Each template includes the format settings, menu arrangements, toolbars, and macros required for creating a certain type of document (such as memoranda or legal briefs).

To select a new template, follow these steps:

1. Open the New Document dialog box by choosing New from the File menu, pressing Ctrl+T, or clicking the New Document button on the WordPerfect 6.1 for Windows toolbar.

2. Select the type of document that you're about to create in the Group list box.

   For example, if you want to design a business card, you select business in the Group list box. If you want to send someone a memorandum, you select Memo in the Group list box. And if you want to send someone a fax, you choose fax in the Group list box.

3. Select the name of the particular template you want to use in the Select Template list box.

   If you want to peek inside the template you chose in the Select Template list box to see how it's laid out, click the View button to open a Viewer window for that template. After opening a Viewer window, you can check out other templates in the selected group simply by clicking their names in succession in the Select Template list box of the New Document dialog box.

Function

Lets you choose the drive containing the document you want to open.

By default, WordPerfect for Windows lists all the files from the current directory in the Filename list box. To restrict the file listing to files of a particular type (such as WordPerfect files with the extension .WPD), choose this option and then select the appropriate type of files in the drop-down list box.

Function

Lets you preview the file selected in the Filename list box in a separate window.

Lets you locate a particular document by searching indexed directories for a file created between a range of dates or containing specific text or word patterns.

Lets you do a bunch of file-related tasks, such as copying, moving, renaming, deleting, or printing the files selected in the Filename list box.

Lets you assign a QuickList alias to a particular directory.

Lets you change the way files are listed in the Filename list box and also lets you designate how much file information will be included in the listing.

Lets you change network settings if you're using WordPerfect 6.1 on a Local Area Network. You don't want to undertake this task unless you've discussed which settings need tweaking with some sort of techie expert or network guru in your organization.

stuff

to open a file not created with WordPerfect for Win-
program opens the Convert File Format dialog box. The
le format is most likely listed in the Convert File Format
box. If the correct format is highlighted, choose OK or
er. Otherwise, choose the correct file format in the drop-
box and choose OK or press Enter.

4. Click the Select button or press Enter to open a new document using the template you just selected.

5. The first time you select a template, WordPerfect 6.1 for Windows prompts you to personalize your template in the Personalize Your Templates dialog box. Choose OK or press Enter to open the Enter Your Personal Information dialog box.

   If you want to personalize the template you're about to open and all future templates that you use, enter the pertinent information in the various fields (like Name, Title, Organization, and so on) of this dialog box. To move to a new field, press Tab or select the Next Field button.

6. When you've finished filling in the different fields, choose OK to close the Personalize Your Templates dialog box. WordPerfect then opens up a template-specific dialog box with fields that supply information used in the particular type of document created by your template.

   For example, if you choose a template for creating a letter, you see the Letter dialog box that contains fields such as the Recipient's Name and Address, the Salutation, and so on. If you open a template for creating a memorandum, WordPerfect displays a Template Information dialog box containing Name of Recipient(s) and Subject fields. Many of these template dialog boxes also contain an Address Book or an Addresses button that takes you to the Template Address Book dialog box, where you can retrieve into the template name-and-address type information about the clients, coworkers, suppliers, and so on that you've stored in the address book simply by selecting their names.

7. After you finish filling in the different fields of the template-specific dialog box, choose OK or press Enter to open a new document using the layout of the selected template and containing the information you entered in these fields.

In addition to using the premade templates that come with WordPerfect 6.1 for Windows, if you're adventurous enough, you can create custom templates of your own. For information on how to do so, refer to Chapter 17 of *WordPerfect For Windows For Dummies.*

More stuff

When you choose <u>N</u>ew from the <u>F</u>ile menu, WordPerfect for Windows opens a new document editing window whose number is indicated on the title bar of the program window (as in `Document1 - unmodified`, `Document2 - unmodified`, and so on). If you have enough memory, WordPerfect for Windows lets you have as many as nine document windows open at one time (proving beyond a shadow of a doubt that you really are overworked!).

See the "Window" section for ways to toggle among open windows and arrange them within a single program window.

Open (Document)

Opens the file you specify into a brand-new document window.

Pull-down menu

For keyb

$Ctrl$ +

For mous

Click on th

The Open

Filename:

Total Files: 0
Total Bytes: 0
Sort: Filename Ascendin
List Files of <u>T</u>ype: All Fil

Option

File<u>n</u>ame

QuickList

<u>D</u>irectories

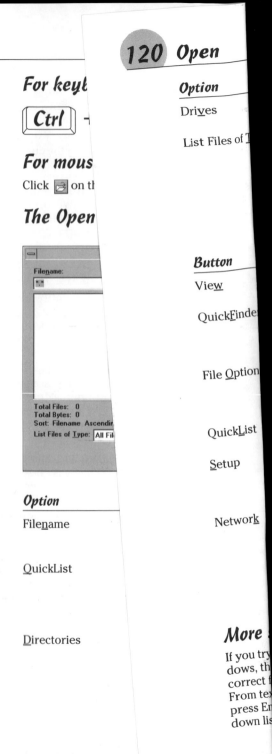

Option

Dri<u>v</u>es

List Files of T

Button

Vie<u>w</u>

Quick<u>F</u>inde

File <u>O</u>ption

Quick<u>L</u>ist

<u>S</u>etup

Networ<u>k</u>

More

If you try
dows, th
correct
From te
press En
down lis

Outline

Creates outlines in your document just like your teacher had you make. When you create an outline, WordPerfect for Windows can automatically number the different levels for you. Then you can combine headings at various levels (as many as eight levels) with regular body text. You can also collapse the outline to hide all the body text so that only the outline headings are displayed, and later you can expand the outline to show everything again.

Pull-down menu

```
Create or edit an outline, or change an outline definition
File  Edit  View  Insert  Format  Table  Graphics  Tools  Window  Help
                                          Spell Check...        Ctrl+F1
                                          Thesaurus...          Alt+F1
Times New Roman    12 pt   Styles    Left    1.0   Grammatik...   Alt+Shift+F1
                                          QuickCorrect... Ctrl+Shift+F1
                                          Language...

                                          Macro                 ▶
                                          Template Macro        ▶

                                          Merge...           Shift+F9
                                          Sort...             Alt+F9
                                          Outline
                                          Hypertext

                                          List
                                          Index
                                          Cross-Reference
                                          Table of Contents
                                          Table of Authorities
                                          Generate...        Ctrl+F9


Insert      HP LaserJet 4 Plus/4M Plus (Win)      Select  November 20, 1994  2:48PM  Pg 1 Ln 1" Pos 1.5"
```

Creating an outline

You can use the outline feature to create formal outlines that would make your English teacher proud. When you create a formal outline, it can have as many as eight successive outline levels. WordPerfect for Windows automatically numbers and formats the entries in each level for you according to the outline style you choose.

To create an outline, just follow these steps:

1. Position the insertion point at the beginning of the line where you want the initial first-level heading of your outline to appear (usually on the first line after the one that contains the name of your outline).

2. Choose Outline from the Tools menu.

   WordPerfect for Windows switches to outline view, displays the Outline feature bar, and inserts the first outline number (1.). The program also indents the insertion point to the first tab stop. (The big, fat 1 you see in the left margin merely indicates that this is a first-level heading.)

3. Type the text of the initial first-level heading and then press Enter.

   WordPerfect for Windows inserts the second outline number (2.) and indents the insertion point so that you can enter the second first-level heading (indicated by the big, fat 1 in the left margin).

4. Type the second, first-level heading and press Enter. If you want to enter the initial second-level heading instead, press Tab to change the outline level (and change from 2. to a. and the big, fat 1 in the left margin to a big, fat 2). Then type the initial, second-level heading and press Enter.

5. WordPerfect for Windows enters the next number (or letter) in sequence for whatever outline level is current. Continue to enter all the headings you want at that level and terminate each one by pressing Enter. Whenever you want to enter a heading for the next-lower level, press Tab to move to the next outline level before entering the heading. Whenever you want to enter a heading at a higher level, press Shift+Tab until you have moved up the levels sufficiently before entering the heading. (Remember that the outline levels are indicated by the big, fat numbers in the left margin.)

6. When you finish entering the last heading for your outline, choose T on the Outline feature bar to convert the last outline number or letter to text (indicated by the big, fat T in the left margin). Then choose Close on the Outline feature bar to switch from outline view and close the Outline feature bar. (As a result, all the big, fat, outline-level numbers in the margin disappear, only to return when you next switch to outline view by choosing Outline from the Tools menu.)

Using the Outline feature bar

When you work with an outline, you can use the buttons on the Outline feature bar to make short work of your outline changes. Remember that WordPerfect for Windows displays the Outline feature bar as soon as you choose Outline from the Tools pull-down menu.

You can use the various buttons on the Outline feature bar to do neat stuff, like change a particular outline heading to the next or preceding outline level, convert regular document text to an outline heading, or convert an outline heading to regular text (with the nifty **T** button). You can also show only particular outline levels between 1 and 8 or None with the Show Outline Levels button or change the outline definition with the Options button.

Although WordPerfect for Windows automatically selects Paragraph, you can choose from several others in the drop-down list. Choose Outline if you want the outline style your teacher taught you: I., II., III., followed by A., B., C., followed by 1., 2., and 3., and so on down the line.

Page Borders (See "Borders")

Page Break

Inserts a *hard* (or manual) *page break* at the insertion point's position. Use this command whenever you want to place some text on a completely new page.

Pull-down menu

```
Begin a new page at the insertion point - Ctrl+Enter
 File  Edit  View  Insert  Format  Table  Graphics  Tools  Window  Help
                    Bullets & Numbers...
                    Character...        Ctrl+W
Times New Roman   12 Abbreviations...            1.0   Tables        Columns        91%
                    Date                      ▶
                    Other                     ▶

                    Footnote                  ▶
                    Endnote                   ▶

                    Comment                   ▶
                    Sound...
                    Bookmark...

                    Spreadsheet/Database      ▶
                    File...
                    Object...
                    Acquire Image...
                    Select Image Source...

                    Page Break    Ctrl+Enter

Insert      HP LaserJet 4 Plus/4M Plus (Win)   Select  November 20, 1994  2:49PM  Pg 1 Ln 1" Pos 1.5"
```

For keyboard kronies

$$\boxed{Ctrl} + \boxed{Enter}$$

More stuff

The secret code for a hard page break you insert in a document is
[HPg]. The secret code for a soft page break that WordPerfect for
Windows automatically inserts in a document is [SPg].

You can delete a hard page break by finding its secret code in the
Reveal Codes window and zapping it. The only way to get rid of a
soft page break is to change the format settings that affect the
number of lines that fit on a page, such as the top and bottom
margins, paper size, or line spacing.

Don't insert hard page breaks until after you have made all your editing changes in the document. Otherwise, when you print the document, you can easily end up with blank pages or pages that have just a little bit of text. Also, remember that WordPerfect for Windows provides a number of commands to keep certain text together on a page no matter how you edit the text.

You don't have to use hard page breaks to keep text from being separated if you utilize these commands (see the section "Keep Text Together").

For more information about this command, see Chapter 10 of *WordPerfect For Windows For Dummies.*

Page Numbering

Adds page numbers to your document, which WordPerfect for Windows automatically keeps up-to-date as you edit.

Pull-down menu

The Page Numbering dialog box

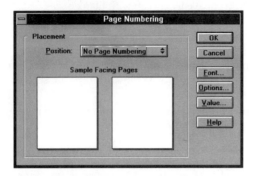

Option or Button	Function
Position	Lets you choose the position of the page numbers (which is then reflected in the Sample Facing Pages area in the Page Numbering dialog box).
Font	Lets you choose a new font, font size, and attribute for the page numbers in the Page Numbering Font dialog box.
Options	Lets you use the Format and Accompanying Text text box to add words to accompany the page number (such as *Page* so that you see Page 1 and Page 2 in the Sample Facing Pages). Lets you include a Secondary Number (such as Page 1, previously Page 2), Chapter Number (such as Chapter 1, Page 1), or Volume Number (such as Volume I, Page 1) in the page numbering by using Insert. Also lets you choose a new type of page numbering for the Page, Secondary, Chapter, and Volume numbers. You can choose Lowercase Letter, Uppercase Letter, Lowercase Roman, or Uppercase Roman.

Option or Button	Function
Value	Lets you change the initial page number for page, secondary, chapter, and volume numbers (either by entering a new number or increasing or decreasing the existing number by a certain amount). Also lets you insert the page, secondary page, chapter, or volume number in the document text at the insertion point.

More stuff

Be sure that the insertion point is somewhere on the first page that is to be numbered (page one if the whole document needs page numbers) before you select the Page Numbering command.

Rather than use the Page Numbering command to number the pages in your document, you can create a header or footer that displays the page number (see the section "Header/Footer").

For more information about this command, see Chapter 10 of *WordPerfect For Windows For Dummies.*

Page View

Displays your entire document and includes margins, headers, footers, page numbers, or footnotes — whatever appears in the top and bottom margin areas. (This is the default view in WordPerfect for Windows.)

Pull-down menu

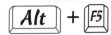

For keyboard kronies

$\boxed{Alt}$ + $\boxed{F5}$

More stuff

Switch to draft view when you want to maximize the amount of text on-screen and don't want to see stuff that's placed in the top and bottom margins.

For more information, refer to the sections "Draft View," "Two Page View," and "Zoom."

For more information about this command, see Chapter 10 of *WordPerfect For Windows For Dummies*.

Paper Size

Lets you choose a new paper size for all pages or particular pages in your document.

Pull-down menu

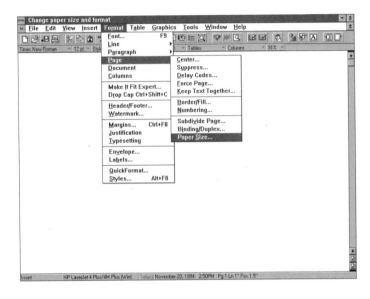

The Paper Size dialog box

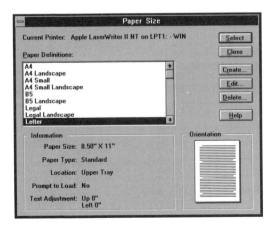

Option or Button	*Function*
P̲aper Definitions	Lets you choose the style of paper you want to use. When you choose a new style in the P̲aper Definitions list box, the program shows you the paper size, location, and orientation (among other things) at the bottom of the Paper Size dialog box.
S̲elect	Selects the paper you have highlighted in the P̲aper Definitions list box and returns you to the document.
C̲reate	Lets you create a new paper definition for your printer in the Create Paper Size dialog box.
E̲dit	Lets you edit the paper definition that's highlighted in the P̲aper Definitions list box.
D̲elete	Lets you delete the paper definition that's highlighted in the Paper D̲efinitions list box.

More stuff

Before you choose a new paper size in the Paper Size dialog box, be sure that the insertion point is somewhere on the page that you're going to change. To change the size of a new page in the document, insert a hard page break by pressing Ctrl+Enter and then change the paper size.

Paragraph Borders (See "Borders")

Paragraph Format

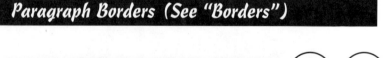

Lets you indent the first line of a paragraph, change the spacing between paragraphs, and adjust the left and right margins of a paragraph (without adjusting the margins of the document).

Pull-down menu

```
Set paragraph formatting options
File  Edit  View  Insert  Format  Table  Graphics  Tools  Window  Help
                          Font...            F9
                          Line              ▶
Times New Roman   12 pt   Paragraph  ▶   Format...
                          Page              Border/Fill...
                          Document
                          Columns           Indent              F7
                                            Hanging Indent    Ctrl+F7
                          Make It Fit Expert...   Double Indent Ctrl+Shift+F7
                          Drop Cap Ctrl+Shift+C   Back Tab

                          Header/Footer...
                          Watermark...

                          Margins...        Ctrl+F8
                          Justification     ▶
                          Typesetting       ▶

                          Envelope...
                          Labels...

                          QuickFormat...
                          Styles...         Alt+F8

Insert      HP LaserJet 4 Plus/4M Plus (Win)   Select November 20, 1994  2:50PM  Pg 1 Ln 1" Pos 1.5"
```

For mouse maniacs

Click 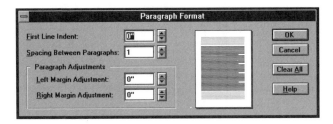 on the WordPerfect 6.1 for Windows toolbar.

The Paragraph Format dialog box

Paragraph Format		
First Line Indent: `0"`		OK
Spacing Between Paragraphs: `1`		Cancel
Paragraph Adjustments		Clear All
Left Margin Adjustment: `0"`		
Right Margin Adjustment: `0"`		Help

Option or Button	Function
First Line Indent	Lets you specify how far to indent only the first line of each paragraph.
Spacing Between Paragraphs	Lets you adjust the spacing between paragraphs (one line by default).
Left Margin Adjustment	Lets you indent the left edge of each paragraph without changing the left margin for the document.
Right Margin Adjustment	Lets you indent the right edge of each paragraph without changing the right margin for the document.
Clear All	Clears all changes made in the Paragraph Format dialog box and returns you to the default settings.

More stuff

Be sure that the insertion point is in the first paragraph you want to adjust before you change the settings in the Paragraph Format dialog box.

If you reach a paragraph in the document in which you want to return to normal formatting, place the insertion point in that paragraph. Then open the Paragraph Format dialog box and choose Clear All.

For more information about this command, see Chapter 9 of *WordPerfect For Windows For Dummies*.

Power Bar

A bar that appears at the top of the program window with buttons on it that you mouse maniacs can use to do common things, such as open, save, or print a document.

Pull-down menu

The buttons on the Power bar

By default, the Power bar contains the following buttons:

Button	Function
Times New Roman — Font Face	Lets you change the font used in the document text (this button shows the current font, as in Times New Roman).
12 pt — Font Size	Lets you change the size of the font used in the document text (this button shows the current font size, as in 12 pt).
Styles — Styles	Lets you select a style for your document (this button shows the name of the current style, or Styles when none is selected).

(continued)

Button	Function
`Left ▾` Justification	Lets you change the justification of the text in the document (this button shows the current justification, as in Left for left justification). See "Justification" for more on changing the text alignment.
`1.0 ▾` Line Spacing	Lets you change the line spacing used in the document text (this button shows the current line spacing, as in 1.0 for single spacing).
`Tables ▾` Tables	Lets you create a table in the document by dragging through a miniature spreadsheet that appears when you double-click its button (this button always shows Tables).
`Columns ▾` Columns	Lets you set up to five newspaper columns in your document (this button shows the current number of newspaper columns, or Columns when newspaper columns are turned off). See "Columns" for more on setting up and using columns in WordPerfect for Windows.
`100% ▾` Zoom	Lets you change magnification of the document text (this button shows the current magnification, as in 100% for actual size).

QuickMenus

To modify the buttons on the Power bar, click the Power bar with the secondary mouse button (the right button if you're a right-handed mouser, or the left button if you're a left-handed mouser) and choose Edit from the QuickMenu. Choose Hide Power Bar from the QuickMenu when you want the Power bar to go away.

More stuff

To find out what a particular button does, position the mouse pointer on the button. WordPerfect for Windows then displays the button's function on the title bar of the program window.

For more information about this command, see Chapter 2 of *WordPerfect For Windows For Dummies.*

Print

Prints all or part of the document located in the current document editing window.

Pull-down menu

Print a document - Ctrl+P
File Edit View Insert Format Table Graphics Tools Window Help
New... Ctrl+T
Open... Ctrl+O
Close Ctrl+F4
Save Ctrl+S
Save As... F3
Master Document ▶
Compare Document ▶
Document Summary...
Document Info...
Print... Ctrl+P
Send ▶
Exit Alt+F4

Insert   HP LaserJet 4 Plus/4M Plus (Win)   Select   November 20, 1994   2:52PM   Pg 1 Ln 1" Pos 1.5"

For keyboard kronies

Ctrl + **P**

For mouse maniacs

Click 🖳 on the WordPerfect 6.1 for Windows toolbar.

The Print dialog box

```
─                              Print
┌─ Current Printer ──────────────────────────┐   ┌─ Print ─┐
│ Apple LaserWriter II NT on LPT1: - WIN      │   │ Close   │
│                              [ Select... ]  │   └─────────┘
└─────────────────────────────────────────────┘   Initialize...
┌─ Print Selection ─┐ ┌─ Copies ──────────────┐   Options...
│ ● Full Document   │ │ Number of Copies: [1][⬍]│  Control
│ ○ Current Page    │ │ Generated By: [WordPerfect ⬍] │
│ ○ Multiple Pages  │ └───────────────────────┘   [ Help ]
│ ○ Selected Text   │ ┌─ Document Settings ───┐
│ ○ Document Summary│ │ Print Quality: [High ⬍]│
│ ○ Document on Disk│ │ Print Color:  [Black ⬍]│
└───────────────────┘ │ ☐ Do Not Print Graphics│
                      └───────────────────────┘
```

Option or Button	Function
Select	Lets you use the Select Printer dialog box to choose a new printer to use (either a printer you installed with Windows or a WordPerfect printer you installed when you installed the program).
Print Selection	Lets you select which section of the document to print. You can choose Full Document (the default), Current Page, Multiple Pages, Selected Text, Document Summary, or Document on Disk.
Copies	Lets you specify the number of copies to print, using the Number of Copies text box. The Generated By pop-up list lets you determine whether WordPerfect generates the copies (they're all collated) or your Printer generates them (you collate them yourself).

Option or Button	*Function*
Document Settings	Lets you change the Print Quality (normally High) and choose a new Print Color (if you're using a color printer). Also lets you omit the printing of graphics by putting an X in the Do Not Print Graphics check box. This option is useful when you want a quick printout and want only to proof the document text.
Initialize	Lets you initialize the printer if you want to clear the printer's memory before printing your document.
Options	Lets you specify some pretty fancy formatting and output printing options. These options include Print in Reverse Order (Back to Front); Print Odd/Even Pages, which prints only the odd or even pages in the document; specifying which output bin to use; and arranging the pages in the chosen bin.
Control	Lets you control the print queue when you print your document on a networked printer.

Printing particular pages

Many times, you want to print only a part of your document. When you select the Multiple Pages radio button in the Print dialog box and choose Print, WordPerfect for Windows displays the Multiple Pages dialog box. This is where you can specify which pages to print.

When you specify the range of pages in this dialog box (secondary pages, chapters, or volumes), be sure to enter the page numbers in numerical order. To specify a range of pages, use a hyphen as follows:

--10	Print from the beginning to page 10
10--	Print from page 10 to the last page
3--10	Print from page 3 to page 10

To specify individual pages, put a comma between the page numbers, as in the following example:

```
4,10,23
```

Only pages 4, 10, and 23 are then printed. You can also combine ranges and individual pages, as in the following example:

```
3-7,9,25
```

Using these commands, only the range of pages 3 through 7 and pages 9 and 23 are printed.

More stuff

When you select <u>P</u>rint to begin a print job, WordPerfect for Windows sends the print job to the WP Print Process program. This program in turn ships it off to the Windows Print Manager. If you want to cancel the printing, you must switch to the WP Print Process or Print Manager window and cancel the printing from there. To switch to either program, click the Control-menu button in the upper-left corner of the WordPerfect for Windows program window and choose S<u>w</u>itch To (or press Ctrl+Esc). Then choose WP Print Process or Print Manager in the Task List dialog box.

For more information about this command, see Chapter 13 of *WordPerfect For Windows For Dummies*.

QuickCorrect

Lets you designate the typos that you routinely make and tell WordPerfect which corrections it should automatically undertake the moment your erring fingers make these boo-boos.

Pull-down menu

```
Correct typing and spelling errors as you type - Ctrl+Shift+F1
File  Edit  View  Insert  Format  Table  Graphics  Tools  Window  Help
                                                   Spell Check...      Ctrl+F1
                                                   Thesaurus...        Alt+F1
Times New Roman    12 pt   Styles      Left    1.0  Grammatik...    Alt+Shift+F1
                                                   QuickCorrect... Ctrl+Shift+F1
                                                   Language...

                                                   Macro              ▶
                                                   Template Macro     ▶

                                                   Merge...          Shift+F9
                                                   Sort...            Alt+F9
                                                   Outline
                                                   Hypertext

                                                   List
                                                   Index
                                                   Cross-Reference
                                                   Table of Contents
                                                   Table of Authorities
                                                   Generate...        Ctrl+F9
```

```
Insert    HP LaserJet 4 Plus/4M Plus (Win)   Select  November 20, 1994   2:52PM  Pg 1 Ln 1" Pos 1.5"
```

For keyboard kronies

$$\boxed{\textit{Ctrl}} + \boxed{\textit{Shift}} + \boxed{\textit{F1}}$$

The QuickCorrect dialog box

```
                              QuickCorrect

Replace:              With:                          Add Entry

[_____]      [_____]              Delete Entry

[c]                   ©                        ▲     Options...
1/2                   ½
acomodate             accommodate                    Close
acsesory              accessory
adn                   and                            Help
adress                address
allready              already
alot                  a lot
antartic              antarctic
aparent               apparent
april                 April
aquaintance           acquaintance
artic                 arctic
asma                  asthma                   ▼

☒ Replace Words as You Type
```

Option or Button	Function
Replace	Type the incorrect spelling that you invariably enter in your document in this text box.
With	In this text box, type the correct (make sure that it's correct) spelling that you want WordPerfect to use whenever you type the incorrect spelling you just entered in the Replace text box.
Add Entry	Click this button to add your new QuickCorrect entry to the list.
Delete Entry	Click this button to remove the selected QuickCorrect entry from its list box.
Options	Click this button to change the sentence and end of sentence QuickCorrect options (such as automatically capitalizing the first letter of a sentence, correcting two capital letters at the start of a word, and reducing double spaces between words to single spaces).
Replace Words as You Type	Keep this check box checked if you want WordPerfect to make corrections as soon as you make the typo. If you deselect this check box, the program will not make your corrections until you spell check the part of the document containing the boo-boo (see "Spell Check" for details on spell checking a document).

QuickFormat

Copies the formatting used in the current paragraph and then allows you to apply this formatting to other selections of text in the document.

Pull-down menu

For mouse maniacs

Click ![icon] on the WordPerfect 6.1 for Windows toolbar.

QuickMenus

Move the insertion point to somewhere in the paragraph that contains the formatting you want to use. Click again, this time with
the secondary mouse button (the right button if you're a right-
handed mouser, or the left button if you're a left-handed mouser),
and choose QuickFormat from the QuickMenu.

Formatting: As easy as selecting text

To use the QuickFormat feature, position the insertion point in
the paragraph whose formatting you want to use elsewhere in the
document. Then choose QuickFormat from the Format pull-down
menu or click anywhere in the text with the secondary mouse
button and choose QuickFormat from the QuickMenu.

WordPerfect for Windows opens the QuickFormat dialog box, where you specify the QuickFormat options you want to use. By default, the program copies the fonts, attributes, and styles used in the original paragraph. If you want to use only the fonts and attributes found in the current paragraph text, choose the Fonts and Attributes radio button. If you want to use only the styles currently in effect, choose the Characters radio button.

When you choose OK or press Enter to close the QuickFormat dialog box, the mouse pointer changes to an I-beam with a paint roller beside it. Use this roller to select all the text you want formatted with the fonts, attributes, and styles found in the original paragraph. As soon as you release the mouse button after selecting the text, the text immediately takes on the font, attribute, and paragraph style formatting used in the original selected paragraph.

More stuff

When you no longer want to use the pointer to "quick" format text, you can change the pointer back to normal. Simply choose QuickFormat from the Format pull-down menu or the text QuickMenu.

QuickMark (see "Bookmark")

QuickMenu

Lets you select commands from a limited pull-down menu that appears when you click an object (such as text or a graphics box) with the secondary mouse button (the right mouse button for right-handers, and the left mouse button for lefties).

More stuff

In WordPerfect for Windows, you can find QuickMenus attached to each of the following screen objects:

- Left margin area of the document (see the section "Select (Text)")

- Top and bottom area of the document (see the section "Header/Footer")

- Menu bar

- Toolbar (see the "Toolbars" section)
- Power bar (see the "Power Bar" section)
- Scroll bars
- Status bar
- Feature bars (see the "Feature Bar" section)
- Document area and document text
- Graphics boxes (see the "Graphics Boxes" section)
- Table cells (see the "Tables" section)

Redline/Strikeout (See "Font")

Repeat

Repeats a keystroke or action, such as moving the insertion point or deleting a character, a set number of times.

Pull-down menu

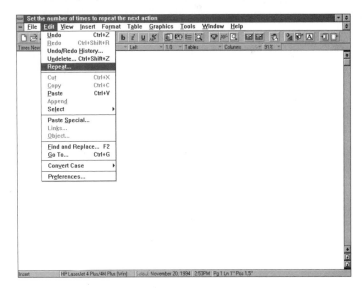

Could you repeat that, please?

Repeat is one of those WordPerfect for Windows features that seems really neat when you first hear about it but is too often overlooked when you're actually editing. WordPerfect for Windows originally added this feature to make it easy to insert a string of characters into your document, such as ———— or ********.

To repeat a character, choose Repeat from the Edit menu and choose OK or press Enter to close the Repeat dialog box. Then type the single character or perform the action you want to repeat.

By default, WordPerfect for Windows repeats eight times the character you type. If you want more or fewer repetitions, type a new number in the Number of Times to Repeat Next Action text box before you choose OK or press Enter. Then type the character to be repeated.

More stuff

You can use the Repeat feature to repeat certain keystrokes and to type characters. You can delete the next eight characters from the insertion point by pressing Delete after opening the Repeat dialog box, for example. Or you can move the insertion point in your document eight characters to the right by pressing the → key. You can move eight pages up in the document by opening the Repeat dialog box and then pressing PgUp.

Reveal Codes

Opens the Reveal Codes window at the bottom of the document editing window. As you edit and format your text, you can view as well as edit all those wacky secret codes WordPerfect for Windows insists on putting in your document.

Pull-down menu

For keyboard kronies

For mouse maniacs

To open the Reveal Codes window with the mouse, position the mouse pointer on either of the two solid, black bars that appear at the very top or bottom of the vertical scroll bar. When the pointer becomes a double-headed arrow pointing up and down, drag the mouse up or down until the border between the regular document window and the Reveal Codes window is where you want it. Then release the mouse button.

To close the Reveal Codes window with the mouse, position the mouse pointer somewhere on the border between the regular document window and the Reveal Codes window. When the pointer becomes an arrow pointing up and down, drag the border all the way up or down until you reach the Power bar or Status bar. Then release the mouse button.

QuickMenus

To modify the appearance of the codes in the Reveal Codes window, click anywhere in the Reveal Codes window with the secondary mouse button (the right mouse button for right-handers and the left mouse button for lefties). Then choose Preferences from the QuickMenu. Choose Hide Reveal Codes from the QuickMenu when you want the Reveal Codes window to go away.

Using Reveal Codes

Reveal Codes gives you a behind-the-scenes look at the placement of all the formatting codes that tell your printer how to produce special effects in your document. You can see codes that define new margin settings, define tabs, center and bold lines of text, set larger font sizes for titles and headings, create paragraph borders around your footer text, and so on.

This information is of absolutely no concern to a normal human being unless, of course, something is wrong with the format of a document and you can't figure how to fix it by using the normal editing window. That's the time when you have to "get under the hood," so to speak, by opening the Reveal Codes window. Then you can edit with all those little secret codes in full view.

When you're editing with the Reveal Codes window open, use the regular document editing window above it to find your general place in the document. Then concentrate on what's happening in the Reveal Codes window to make your changes. You mouse maniacs can use the mouse to reposition the Reveal Codes cursor in the Reveal Codes window by simply clicking the mouse pointer where you want it to be. (It's not really an insertion point in this window because it appears as a red block.)

To delete a code, position the Reveal Codes cursor either directly in front of or behind the code. If the cursor is in front of the code, press Delete to get rid of it. If the cursor is behind the code, press Backspace to back over the code and delete it. If you're using the mouse, you can remove a code by selecting it and then dragging it until the pointer is outside the Reveal Codes window. Then you can release the mouse button.

More stuff

You can change the normal size of the codes in addition to other appearance options. To do so, choose Preferences from the Edit pull-down menu and double-click the Display icon. Then choose the Reveal Codes radio button in the Display Preferences dialog box. You can change all the settings you want, including the font and font size of the text or any of the settings in the Options area that control the appearance of the codes in the Reveal Codes window. You can also change the size of the Reveal Codes window.

For more information about this command, see Chapter 11 of *WordPerfect For Windows For Dummies.*

Ruler Bar

The ruler bar shows the current settings of the tabs and the left and right margins at the insertion point. You can manipulate the tab and margin icons to change these settings.

Pull-down menu

For keyboard kronies

For mouse maniacs

Double-click the tab ruler on the ruler bar to bring up the Display Preferences dialog box. Double-click a tab icon on the tab ruler to display the Tab Set dialog box. Double-click the left- or right-margin icon or the white space between them above the tab ruler to display the Margins dialog box. Double-click the triangles next to the left- and right-margin icons (representing the paragraph margins) to display the Paragraph Format dialog box.

To change the left or right margin settings, drag the left- or right-margin icon above the tab ruler. To change the left indent of your paragraphs, drag the bottom triangle that points left. (Both the top and bottom triangles move together.) To change the right indent of the paragraphs, drag the bottom triangle that points right so that it's next to the right-margin icon. To change the indent of only the first line of the paragraphs, drag just the top triangle that points left.

To change a tab setting, drag the tab icon to a new position on the tab ruler. To remove a tab setting, drag the tab icon off the tab ruler. To add a new tab, select the type of tab (Left, Center, Right, Decimal, ...Left, ...Center, ...Right, or ...Decimal) on the Ruler Bar QuickMenu and then click the place on the tab ruler where you want this tab to be added.

QuickMenus

You can use the QuickMenu associated with the ruler bar to change the tab settings, change that paragraph format, adjust margins, set columns, or create tables. You can also use the QuickMenu to hide the ruler bar or change the ruler bar display preferences. To open the QuickMenu, click anywhere in the area of the ruler bar, which is marked by the left- and right-margin icons above the tab ruler.

You can use the QuickMenu associated with each tab to select a new type of tab, clear all tabs from the ruler, change the tab settings in the Tab Set dialog box, or hide the ruler bar or change the ruler bar display preferences. To open this QuickMenu, click anywhere on a tab icon with the secondary mouse button (the right mouse button for right-handers, and the left mouse button for lefties).

More stuff

You can also change the margin settings by using the Margins dialog box and your tab settings by using the Tab Set dialog box. (See the sections "Margins" and "Tab Set" for more information.)

For more information about this command, see Chapter 2 of *WordPerfect For Windows For Dummies*.

Save

Lets you save your changes to a document on disk so that you have a copy of the document for future use. The first time you save, you must give the document a new filename. After that, you can use this command to save your changes to that file as you continue to work.

Pull-down menu

Save the current document - Ctrl+S

| File | Edit | View | Insert | Format | Table | Graphics | Tools | Window | Help |

New...	Ctrl+T
Open...	Ctrl+O
Close	Ctrl+F4
Save	Ctrl+S
Save As...	F3
Master Document	▶
Compare Document	▶
Document Summary...	
Document Info...	
Print...	Ctrl+P
Send	▶
Exit	Alt+F4

Insert   HP LaserJet 4 Plus/4M Plus (Win)   Select   November 20, 1994   2:54PM   Pg 1 Ln 1" Pos 1.5"

For keyboard kronies

[**Ctrl**] + [**S**]

For mouse maniacs

Click  on the WordPerfect 6.1 for Windows toolbar to save your document.

Saving a file for the first time

To save a file for the first time, you have to go through the whole rigmarole described in this section. After that, however, you only have to choose Save from the File menu to save your changes. (WordPerfect for Windows doesn't bother with filenames, passwords, and that kind of stuff.) To initially save your file, follow these steps:

1. Choose Save from the File menu or press Ctrl+S; the program displays the Save As dialog box.

2. By using the Drives drop-down list box, the QuickList, or the Directories list box, select the drive and directory in which you want the file to be saved.

3. Type the name for your new file in the Filename text box. The main filename can be as long as eight characters and the (optional) filename extension can be as long as three characters. The extension is separated from the main filename with a period.

4. To assign a password to your file, choose the Password Protect option to put an X in its check box.

5. Choose OK or press Enter to save the document.

6. If you checked the Password Protect box, the Password dialog box appears. Type the password just as you want it recorded and differentiate uppercase from lowercase letters. (Notice that WordPerfect for Windows masks each character you type.) Choose OK or press Enter. You must then retype the password exactly as you originally typed it and again choose OK or press Enter.

   If you mess up and type the password a little differently the second time, WordPerfect for Windows displays a dialog box which lets you know that the passwords don't match and lets you try again after choosing OK or pressing Enter to clear the Alert dialog box.

More stuff

Spare yourself lots of heartbreak and wasted time by saving your documents often. Save every time you are interrupted (by the telephone, your boss, or whatever) and save whenever you have made more changes to the document than you would ever want to have to redo.

Save As

Lets you change the name or location of your WordPerfect for Windows document. You can even save your document in a different file format. This way, coworkers less fortunate than you who have to use some other word processor can have access to your document.

Pull-down menu

For keyboard kronies

[F3]

The Save As dialog box

```
┌─────────────────────── Save As ───────────────────────┐
│ Filename:          c:\office\wpwin\wpdocs    ┌─────────┐│
│ ┌──────────────┐ ▼                           │   OK    ││
│ │*.*           │   QuickList:                 └─────────┘│
│ └──────────────┘   ┌──────────────────────┐  ┌─────────┐│
│ ┌──────────────┐   │Documents             │  │ Cancel  ││
│ │              │   │Graphics Directory    │  └─────────┘│
│ │              │   │Macro Directory       │  ┌─────────┐│
│ │              │   │Printer Directory     │  │ View... ││
│ │              │   │Template Directory    │  └─────────┘│
│ │              │   └──────────────────────┘  │QuickFinder...│
│ │              │   Directories:               │File Options ▼│
│ │              │   ┌──────────────────────┐  │QuickList  ▼ │
│ │              │   │📁 c:\                 │  │ Setup... ││
│ │              │   │  📁 office            │  │Network... ▼│
│ │              │   │    📁 wpwin           │  ┌─────────┐│
│ │              │   │      📁 wpdocs        │  │  Help   ││
│ └──────────────┘   └──────────────────────┘  └─────────┘│
│ Total Files: 0    Drives:   690,464 KB Free            │
│ Total Bytes: 0    ┌──────────────────────┐             │
│ Sort: Filename Ascending │ c:          ▼  │             │
│ Save File as Type: │WordPerfect 6.0/6.1 [*.wpd;*.wpt;*.doc ▼│
│                              □ Password Protect         │
└────────────────────────────────────────────────────────┘
```

Option	Function
File<u>n</u>ame	Lets you change the filename of your document. To make a copy under the same filename but in a new directory, just type a new pathname and leave the filename unchanged.
QuickList	Lets you change to the directory in which the document is saved by selecting the alias that you gave the directory name in the QuickList list box.
<u>D</u>irectories	Lets you change the directory, if you want to save the file in a directory other than the current one.
Dri<u>v</u>es	Lets you change the drive if you want to save the file on a disk in a different drive.

Option	**Function**
Save File as <u>T</u>ype	Lets you save the document in another file format. (WordPerfect 6.1 For Windows supports a bunch.) Just select the new format type in the drop-down list.
<u>P</u>assword Protect	Lets you password-protect your file. Don't mess with a password unless you are really sure that you won't forget it. (It's a good idea to write down any passwords and store them in a secure place. This way, coworkers can get into your files if you suddenly decide to chuck it all and live in Tahiti.)

Button	**Function**
Vie<u>w</u>	Lets you preview in a separate window the contents of the file that is selected in the File<u>n</u>ame list box.
Quick<u>F</u>inder	Lets you locate a particular document by searching indexed directories for a file created between a range of dates or containing specific text or word patterns.
File <u>O</u>ptions	Lets you perform tasks to the files selected in the File<u>n</u>ame list box, such as copying, moving, renaming, deleting, or printing.
Quick<u>L</u>ist	Lets you assign a QuickList alias to a particular directory.
<u>S</u>etup	Lets you change the way files are listed in the File<u>n</u>ame list box and lets you designate how much file information you want to include in the list.
Networ<u>k</u>	Lets you change network settings if you're using WordPerfect 6.1 for Windows on a Local Area Network. This is not something you want to undertake unless you've discussed what settings need tweaking with some sort of techie expert or network guru in your organization.

More stuff

Use <u>S</u>ave from the <u>F</u>ile menu when you want to save editing and
formatting changes to the document and update the file. Use Save
<u>A</u>s to save the document with a new filename or in a new direc-
tory, in another file format for use with another word processor,
or if someone convinces you that you need to add a password to
the document.

For more information about this command, see Chapter 15 of
WordPerfect For Windows For Dummies.

Search and Replace (See "Find and Replace")

Select (Text)

Marks a section of text so that you can do all sorts of neat things
to it, such as cut and paste it, spell-check it, print it, or even get
rid of it.

Pull-down menu

For keyboard kronies

QuickMenus

Click the secondary mouse pointer (the right mouse button for right-handers, and the left mouse button for lefties) in the left margin area of the document. Then choose one of the following: Select S̲entence to select the current sentence; Select P̲aragraph to select the current paragraph; Select P̲age to select the current page; or Select A̲ll to select the entire document.

For mouse maniacs

Position the mouse pointer in front of the first character of text that is to be highlighted and drag the pointer through the entire block of text. To select the current word, double-click somewhere in the word. To select the current paragraph, triple-click somewhere in the paragraph. To select a block of text, click the insertion point in front of the first character, press and hold Shift, and then click the last character. WordPerfect for Windows highlights all the text in between.

Marking selections keyboard-style

To mark a selection with the keyboard, follow these steps:

1. Position the insertion point in front of the first character to be included in the selection.

2. Press F8 or press and hold Shift. The Select indicator on the Status bar becomes activated.

3. Use the insertion-point movement keys to extend the selection (see the section "Insertion Point" for details). WordPerfect for Windows highlights all the text you cover as you move the insertion point.

Other slick ways to extend a block

WordPerfect for Windows offers all sorts of fast ways to extend a selected block after you have turned on blocking. This list shows a few shortcuts you might want to try:

• Press Ctrl+→ to extend the block to the next word to the right or Ctrl+←to extend the block to the next word to the left.

- Press ↑ to extend the block up one line. Press ↓ to extend the block down one line.

- Press Ctrl+Home to extend the selection from the insertion point to the beginning of the document or Ctrl+End to extend it from the insertion point to the end of the document.

More stuff

If you ever find yourself selecting the wrong text, you can cancel the selection by pressing F8 or by clicking the insertion point anywhere in the document.

Show ¶

Displays symbols on the screen for each code you have entered in your document, including hard return, space, tab, indent, centering, flush right, soft hyphen, center page, and advance.

Pull-down menu

For keyboard kronies

$\boxed{Ctrl}$ + $\boxed{Shift}$ + $\boxed{F3}$

More stuff

You can define which codes are to be represented by symbols on the screen by choosing Preferences from the Edit menu and then choosing Display. In the Display Preferences dialog box, choose the Show ¶ radio button. In the Symbols to Display area, deselect any of the check box options that you don't want displayed when Show ¶ from the View menu is activated.

Sort

Lets you rearrange text in alphabetic or numeric order. In Word-Perfect for Windows, you can sort lines of text (such as simple lists), paragraphs, records in a merge text data file, or rows in a table (see the sections "Merge" and "Tables" for more information).

Pull-down menu

For keyboard kronies

Sorting information in WordPerfect for Windows

Sorting is based on keys, which indicate what specific information should be used to alphabetize or numerically reorder the text. You might have a list that contains your coworkers' names and telephone numbers, for example, and you want to sort the list alphabetically by last name. You tell WordPerfect for Windows to use the last name of each person as the sorting key. When you sort information with WordPerfect for Windows, you can define more than one sorting key. If your list of names and telephone numbers contains several Smiths and Joneses, you can define a second key that indicates how you want the duplicates to be arranged (by first name, for example).

To sort information in WordPerfect for Windows, follow these steps:

1. Open the document that contains the information you want to sort by choosing Open from the File menu.

2. If you want to sort a table or parallel columns, position the insertion point somewhere in the table or the columns. If you want to sort specific lines or paragraphs in a document, select just the lines or paragraphs (see the section "Select (Text)" for more information).

3. Choose Sort from the Tools menu (or press Alt+F9) to open the Sort dialog box.

4. If you want to save the sorted information in a file other than the current document file, use the Output File option to indicate which file to use.

5. Select the type of sort you want to use (such as First word in a line) in the Defined Sorts list box.

6. If you want uppercase letters sorted before lowercase letters, choose Uppercase First in the Options pop-up menu to put a checkmark in front of the option.

7. If you want to be able to restore your document to its original order by choosing Undo (Ctrl+Z) after sorting it, choose Allow Undo in the Options pop-up menu to put a checkmark in front of the option.

8. Choose Sort or press Enter to begin sorting.

Defining all sorts of new sorts

WordPerfect 6.1 ships the definitions for the most common types of sorts that you may use. In some situations, you may have to create your own sort definition, as follows:

1. Choose Sort from the Tools menu (or press Alt+F9) to open the Sort dialog box.

2. Choose the New button in the Sort dialog box to open the New Sort dialog box.

3. Replace ⟨User Defined Sort⟩ in the Sort Name text box with the name of the sort you're defining, which you want to appear in the Defined Sorts list box of the Sort dialog box.

4. If necessary, change the type of sort by choosing the appropriate radio button under Sort By. You can sort by Line, Paragraph, Merge Record, Table Row, or Column.

5. Define the first key by making any necessary changes to the Type, Sort Order, Field, Line, Word, and Cell (when you're performing a Table sort) settings for Key 1.

By default, WordPerfect for Windows performs an Alpha sort in ascending order (from A to Z) based on the first word in the first line of the first field (or cell, when you're performing a Table sort).

6. To sort by another key, choose Add Key. Then change any of the settings that need modifying for Key 2.

7. Repeat step 6 until you have defined all the sort keys you want. (Extra keys are necessary only when the previous key has duplicates and you want to tell WordPerfect for Windows how to treat them — such as sorting by first name when you have duplicate last names.)

8. Choose OK or press Enter to close the New Sort dialog box and return to the Sort dialog box, where your new sort definition is displayed in the Defined Sorts list box.

9. To use the new definition in sorting, make sure it's selected in the Defined Sorts list box; then choose Sort. To return to your document without using the new sort definition, choose Close instead.

More stuff

The "key" to understanding sorting in WordPerfect for Windows is to understand that the program divides information into fields and records, based on different types of sorts, as shown in this list:

- In a <u>L</u>ine sort, each line terminated by a hard return is considered to be a record. These records can be subdivided into fields (separated by tabs) and words (separated by spaces, slashes, or hyphens).

- In a <u>P</u>aragraph sort, each paragraph that ends in two or more hard returns is a record. These records can be subdivided into lines (separated by soft returns), fields (separated by tabs), and words (separated by spaces, slashes, or hyphens).

- In a <u>M</u>erge Record sort, each record ends with an ENDRECORD merge code. These records can be subdivided into fields (separated by ENDFIELD codes), lines (separated by hard returns), and words (separated by spaces, slashes, or hyphens).

- In a (Parallel) <u>C</u>olumn sort, each record is one row of parallel columns. (See the "Columns" section for definitions of types of columns.) These records can be subdivided into columns (separated by a hard page), lines (separated by soft or hard returns), and words (separated by spaces, slashes, or hyphens).

- In a <u>T</u>able sort, each record is one row. These records can be subdivided into cells (numbered from left to right beginning with one), lines (separated by hard returns), and words (separated by spaces, slashes, or hyphens).

Spell Check

Lets you eliminate all those embarrassing spelling errors. The WordPerfect for Windows Spell Checker also locates double words (repeated words) and words with weird capitalization.

Pull-down menu

```
Check for misspelled words, double words, irregular capitalization - Ctrl+F1
 File  Edit  View  Insert  Format  Table  Graphics  Tools  Window  Help
                                                     Spell Check...      Ctrl+F1
                                                     Thesaurus...        Alt+F1
Times New Roman    12 pt  Styles          Left    1.0  Grammatik...    Alt+Shift+F1
                                                     QuickCorrect... Ctrl+Shift+F1
                                                     Language...

                                                     Macro                    ▶
                                                     Template Macro           ▶

                                                     Merge...           Shift+F9
                                                     Sort...              Alt+F9
                                                     Outline
                                                     Hypertext

                                                     List
                                                     Index
                                                     Cross-Reference
                                                     Table of Contents
                                                     Table of Authorities
                                                     Generate...          Ctrl+F9




Insert        HP LaserJet 4 Plus/4M Plus (Win)   Select November 20, 1994  2:56PM  Pg 1 Ln 1" Pos 1.5"
```

For keyboard kronies

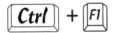

For mouse maniacs

Click 🖰 on the WordPerfect 6.1 for Windows toolbar.

Spell checking a document

To check the spelling in your document, follow these steps:

1. To check the spelling of a word or page, position the insertion point somewhere in that word or on that page. To
   check the spelling from a particular word in the text to the
   end of the document, position the insertion point on that
   word. To check the spelling of the entire document, you can
   position the insertion point anywhere in the document.

2. Choose Spell Check from the Tools menu (or press Ctrl+F1)
   to open the Spell Check window.

3. By default, the program spell checks the entire document (unless text is selected, in which case the program opts to check only the selection). To change the amount of text that is spell checked, choose the appropriate command from the Check pull-down menu in the Spell Check menu bar. The commands for specific text are Word; Sentence; Paragraph; Page; Document; To End of Document; Selected Text; Text Entry Box; or Number of Pages.

4. Choose Start or press Enter to begin spell checking.

When the Spell Check locates a word it cannot find in its dictionary, the Spell Check highlights the word in the text and displays the word at the top of the Spell Check window after the Not found message. The Spell Check then lists all suggestions for replacing the unknown (and potentially misspelled) word in the Suggestions list box. The first suggestion in this list is also shown in the Replace With text box.

5. To replace the unknown word with the word located in the Replace With text box, choose Replace or press Enter. To replace the unknown word with another proposed word from the Suggestions list box, select the proposed word. After it appears in the Replace With text box, choose Replace or press Enter.

To skip the unknown word one time only and continue spell checking, choose Skip Once.

To skip this unknown word and every other occurrence of it throughout the document, choose Skip Always.

To add the unknown word to the supplementary spelling dictionary (so that the Spell Check skips the word in this and every other document), choose Add.

To edit the unknown word while in the text, click the word in the document to activate the document window. Then make your changes. When you're ready to resume spell checking, choose Resume in the Spell Check window.

There may be no suggestions for the unknown word offered in the Replace With text box and Suggestions list box. Or maybe none of the suggestions is anywhere close to the word you tried to spell. If this occurs, enter a best-guess spelling in the Replace With text box and then choose Suggest to have the Spell Check look up the word.

6. When the Spell Check locates the occurrence of a duplicate word in the text, it highlights both words and suggests just one of the words as the replacement in the Replace With text box. To disable duplicate word checking, choose Duplicate Words from the Options pull-down menu on the Spell Check menu bar.

7. When the Spell Check locates a word that uses irregular capitalization, it highlights this word and makes various alternative capitalization suggestions in the Replace With text box and Suggestions list box. To disable irregular capitalization checking, choose Irregular Capitalization from the Options pull-down menu on the Spell Check menu bar.

8. When the Spell Check encounters a word with numbers in it (such as B52 or RX7), the Spell Check highlights the unknown word and displays whatever suggestions it can come up with in the Replace With text box and Suggestions list box. To disable spell checking of words with numbers, choose Words with Numbers from the Options pull-down menu on the Spell Check menu bar.

9. When the Spell Check finishes checking the document (or the part you indicated), it displays a Spell Check dialog box informing you that the spell check has been completed and asks whether you want to close the Spell Check. Choose Yes or press Enter to close the Spell Check window and return to the document. You can also close the Spell Check at any time by choosing Close or double-clicking its Control-menu button.

More stuff

Save your document immediately after spell checking it to ensure that you don't lose the edits made by way of the Spell Check. For more information about this command, see Chapter 7 of *WordPerfect For Windows For Dummies*.

Status Bar

Keeps you informed of lots of useful information like whether you're in Insert or Typeover mode, which printer is selected, the current date and time, and the current page, line, and cursor position.

Pull-down menu

For mouse maniacs

To hide the Status bar, click the Status bar with the secondary mouse button and then choose Hide Status Bar from the QuickMenu.

More stuff

You can change what information is displayed on the Status bar and how it is displayed by choosing Preferences on the Status bar QuickMenu. To add or remove items, select or deselect their check boxes in the Status Bar Items list box. To rearrange the order of the items on the Status bar, drag their buttons to new positions. To resize an item, position the mouse pointer on the item's border and, when the pointer changes to a double-headed arrow, drag the border in the appropriate direction. To change the font and font size used on the Status bar, choose the Options button and then select the desired font face and font size in the Font and Size list boxes, respectively.

Styles

Lets you format various parts of a document in the same manner by simply applying the appropriate style to the text. By using styles, you don't have to use individual formatting commands every time you format text.

Pull-down menu

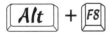

For keyboard kronies

Alt + **F8**

Styles à la QuickStyle

You can create a style for your document by choosing each format setting from the WordPerfect for Windows pull-down menu in the Style Editor. The easiest way to create the style, however, is by example using the QuickCreate feature, as shown in these steps:

1. Format the document text exactly as you want it to appear in the style, including fonts, sizes, attributes, alignment, justification, and so on.

2. Select the formatted text. Be sure to include as part of your selection all the secret codes that change the font or font size or otherwise format this selected text!

3. Choose Styles from the Format menu (or press Alt+F8) to open the Style List dialog box.

4. Choose QuickStyle to open the QuickStyle dialog box.

5. Enter a name for your new style (such as 1st Head) in the Style Name text box. The name can be as long as 12 characters. Then press Tab.

6. Enter a description of the new style (such as 50-point bold Helvetica) in the Description text box.

7. By default, WordPerfect for Windows creates a Paragraph style. This means that the program applies the formatting to the entire paragraph. To create a Character style instead (the program applies the formatting to only the selected text), choose the Character radio button.

8. Choose OK or press Enter to close the QuickStyle dialog box and return to the Style List dialog box. Your new style is now listed and selected.

9. To apply your brand-new style to the text that is currently selected in the document, choose Apply. To close the Style List dialog box without assigning the style to the selected text, choose Close.

More stuff

To turn on a style before you type the text, position the insertion point in the text where you want the style formatting to begin. Then open the Style List dialog box by choosing Styles from the Format menu or by pressing Alt+F8. Select the style in the Name list box and choose Apply or press Enter. Now you can type the text. To turn off the style in a new paragraph, open the Style List dialog box and select <None> in the Name list box. Then choose Apply or press Enter.

To apply a paragraph style to an existing paragraph of text, position the insertion point somewhere in that paragraph. Then select the style in the Name list box found in the Style List dialog box and choose Apply or press Enter.

For more information about this command, see Chapter 12 of *WordPerfect For Windows For Dummies.*

Suppress

Lets you temporarily stop the printing of a header, footer, or page number on a single page of the document.

Pull-down menu

```
Turn off headers, footers, etc., for the current page
 File  Edit  View  Insert  Format  Table  Graphics  Tools  Window  Help

Times New Roman    12 pt   Style              Tables        Column       91%

                    Font...              F9
                    Line
                    Paragraph
                    Page              Center...
                    Document          Suppress...
                    Columns           Delay Codes...
                                      Force Page...
                    Make It Fit Expert...   Keep Text Together...
                    Drop Cap Ctrl+Shift+C
                    Header/Footer...   Border/Fill...
                    Watermark...       Numbering...
                    Margins...  Ctrl+F8  Subdivide Page...
                    Justification      Binding/Duplex...
                    Typesetting        Paper Size...
                    Envelope...
                    Labels...
                    QuickFormat...
                    Styles...  Alt+F8

Insert      HP LaserJet 4 Plus/4M Plus (Win)   Select  November 20, 1994  2:58PM  Pg 1 Ln 1" Pos 1.5"
```

This header is suppressed!

Suppress lets you stop page numbering, headers, footers, or watermarks from printing on a particular page. To do so, just open the Suppress dialog box and choose the check boxes for all the page elements that should not appear on the current page.

When you're suppressing normal page numbering on the current page, you can choose the Print Page Number at Bottom Center on Current Page option by putting an X in its check box. This option prints the page number in the center near the bottom of just that single page.

More stuff

Before choosing this command, position the insertion point some-where on the page where you want the page elements to be tem-porarily suspended.

For more information about this command, see Chapter 10 of *WordPerfect For Windows For Dummies*.

Tab Set

Lets you change the tabs in your document.

Pull-down menu

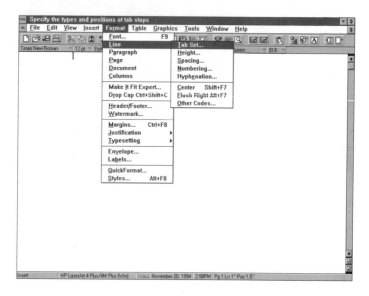

QuickMenus

You can change the tabs by using the Tab Set dialog box. To do so, click the ruler bar (displayed by choosing <u>R</u>uler Bar from the <u>V</u>iew menu) with the secondary mouse button (the right mouse button for right-handers, and the left mouse button for lefties).

For mouse maniacs

You can change tabs directly on the ruler bar (see the "Ruler Bar" section for details). You can also display the Tab Set dialog box and change the tabs by double-clicking any of the tab icons displayed on the ruler bar.

The changing of the tabs

Tab Set

Settings

Type: Left   Position: 0"

☐ Repeat Every: 0.500"

Position From

◉ Left Margin (Relative)   ◯ Left Edge of Paper (Absolute)

Dot Leader Options

Dot Leader Character: .

Spaces Between Characters: 1

Align Character

Character: .

OK   Cancel   Set   Clear   Clear All   Default   Help

You can change tabs anywhere in the document text. To set uniform tabs for the document, follow these steps:

1. Position the insertion point somewhere in the first paragraph where the new tab settings will take effect.

2. Choose Line from the Format menu and then choose Tab Set from the cascading menu to open the Tab Set dialog box.

3. Choose Clear All to delete all the current tabs.

4. Select the type of tabs you want to set in the Type pop-up list (Left, Center, Right, Decimal, Dot Left, Dot Center, Dot Right, or Dot Decimal).

5. Choose Position and enter the distance between the first tab and the left margin or the left edge of the page. You can also select this distance with the up- and down-arrow buttons. Zero inches puts the first tab in line with the left margin.

6. Choose Repeat Every by putting an X in its check box and, using its text box, enter a measurement for how far apart each tab stop should be. You can also select this measurement with the up- and down-arrow buttons.

7. If you want the tabs to always remain fixed, even if you change the left margin, select the Left Edge of Paper (Absolute) radio button. Otherwise, the Left Margin (Relative) radio button is chosen by default.

8. To change the dot leader character when you're using a dot leader tab (such as Dot Left, Dot Center, Dot Right, or Dot Decimal), choose Dot Leader Character. Then enter the new character in the text box. To insert a character not available from the keyboard, press Ctrl+W and choose the WordPerfect Character (see the "WordPerfect Characters" section).

   To change the spacing between each dot, choose Space Between Characters and then enter the new distance in the text box. (Or you can select this measurement with the up- and down-arrow buttons.)

9. To change the alignment character when you're setting Decimal or Dot Decimal tabs, choose Character under Align Character and enter the new alignment characters in the text box.

10. Choose Set to move the insertion point to the end of the first tab measurement. Put an X in the Repeat Every check box, enter the distance that should separate each subsequent tab in its text box, and press Enter. As soon as you choose Set, WordPerfect for Windows uses the separation interval in the Repeat Every text box to indicate the location of the tabs across the ruler with the appropriate letters. You can also see the new tab settings take effect in your document text by looking at the text that shows behind the Tab Set dialog box.

11. Choose OK or press Enter to close the Tab Set dialog box and return to your document. You can now see your new uniform tab settings.

More stuff

You can also set individual tab settings in the Tab Set dialog box. Simply choose the type of tab and enter its position (relative to the left margin or the left edge of the paper) in the Position text box. Then choose Set to insert the tab on the tab ruler.

Keep in mind that instead of going through the rigmarole of changing tabs in the Tab Set dialog box, you can change the tabs on the ruler bar (see the "Ruler Bar" section for more information).

...

Tables **171**

For more information about this command, see Chapter 9 of
WordPerfect For Windows For Dummies.

Tables

Lets you set text in a tabular format by using a layout of columns
and rows, much like a spreadsheet. Tables not only superficially
resemble spreadsheets, in fact, but they can also accommodate
worksheets created with that type of software and can perform
most of the same functions. Moreover, the boxes formed by the
intersection of a column and a row are called *cells,* just as they
are in a spreadsheet. Each cell has a cell address that corre-
sponds to the letter of its column (from A to Z and then doubled,
as in AA, AB, and so on) and the number of its row (the first row
is 1). Therefore, the first cell in the upper left corner is A1 (because it's in column A and row 1).

Pull-down menu

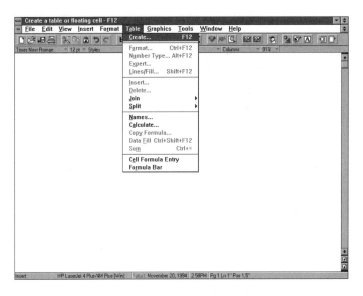

For keyboard kronies

For mouse maniacs

 Click the Tables button on the Power bar (see "Power Bar" for details) and drag through the tiny table grid until you have highlighted all the cells you want in the table. Then release the mouse button.

To change the width of a column in a table, position the mouse pointer somewhere on the border of the column you want to change. When the pointer changes to a double-headed arrow pointing to the left and right, drag the column border until the column is the width you want.

 When you create a new table (or position the insertion point in any of the cells in an existing table), WordPerfect for Windows automatically switches to the Tables toolbar, which contains lots of useful buttons (such as Table Expert, Table Format, Lines/Fill, Number Type, and so on) for formatting the new table.

QuickMenus

The Table QuickMenu enables you to do lots of table-related stuff, such as format existing cells or insert or delete cells. You can also use the QuickMenu to display the formula bar when you create and calculate formulas in the cells.

Creating a table

To create a table, first indicate the number of columns and rows the table should have by following these steps:

1. Move the insertion point to the beginning of the new line in the document where you want the table to appear.

2. Choose Create from the Table menu or press F12 to open the Create Table dialog box.

3. By default, WordPerfect for Windows creates a table with three columns and one row. To accept this default table size, choose OK or press Enter. To create a table that has more columns and rows, enter the number of columns in the Columns text box and the number of rows in the Rows text box. Then choose OK or press Enter.

Entering text in a table

After creating the table structure, you can enter text in the various cells of the table. To enter text, position the insertion point in the cell (it's in the first cell by default) and begin typing. To advance to the next cell on the right, press Tab. To return to the previous cell, press Shift+Tab (which is a backward tab). When you reach the last cell in a row, pressing Tab moves you to the cell at the beginning of the next row. If you press Tab when the insertion point is in the last cell of a table, WordPerfect for Windows adds a blank row of cells to the table and positions the insertion point in the first cell in this new row.

More stuff

You can convert a table created with tabs or parallel columns into a WordPerfect for Windows table (see the "Columns" section for more information about parallel columns). To do so, select the lines of the tabular table or parallel columns and choose Create from the Table menu, which opens the Convert Table dialog box. Then choose either the Tabular Column or Parallel Column radio button under Create Table From and choose OK or press Enter.

For more information about this command, see Chapter 16 of *WordPerfect For Windows For Dummies.*

Thesaurus

Lets you find synonyms (words with similar meanings) and antonyms (words with opposite meanings) for many of the words you overuse in a document.

Pull-down menu

```
Display synonyms and antonyms for a word - Alt+F1
File  Edit  View  Insert  Format  Table  Graphics    Tools  Window  Help
                                                    Spell Check...      Ctrl+F1
                                                    Thesaurus...         Alt+F1
Times New Roman  ▼ 12 pt ▼ Styles      ▼ Left   ▼ 1.0  Grammatik...  Alt+Shift+F1
                                                    QuickCorrect... Ctrl+Shift+F1
                                                    Language...

                                                    Macro                    ▶
                                                    Template Macro           ▶

                                                    Merge...          Shift+F9
                                                    Sort...            Alt+F9
                                                    Outline
                                                    Hypertext

                                                    List
                                                    Index
                                                    Cross-Reference
                                                    Table of Contents
                                                    Table of Authorities
                                                    Generate...       Ctrl+F9

Insert          HP LaserJet 4 Plus/4M Plus (Win)   Select  November 20, 1994  2:59PM  Pg 1 Ln 1" Pos 1"
```

For keyboard kronies

Alt + **F8**

More stuff

To look up a word in the Thesaurus, position the insertion point somewhere in the word and then open the Thesaurus dialog box (press Alt+F1).

Keep in mind that when you replace a word with a synonym or antonym from the Thesaurus, WordPerfect for Windows makes no attempt to match the original tense or number in the text. So if you look up the word *jumped* in a document and select *leap* in the Thesaurus dialog box as its replacement, WordPerfect for Windows inserts *leap* without an *ed* (which you must then add yourself).

For more information about this command, see Chapter 7 of *WordPerfect For Windows For Dummies*.

Toolbars

Let you select WordPerfect 6.1 for Windows commands, insert stock text, launch new programs, or play macros by simply displaying the correct toolbar and then clicking the correct button. (In previous versions of WordPerfect for Windows, toolbars were known as Button bars.)

Pull-down menu

To display or hide the selected toolbar, choose the following View menu command:

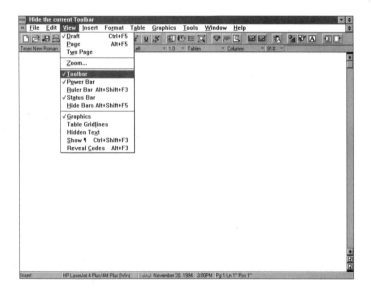

For mouse maniacs

To display a new toolbar, click the currently displayed toolbar with the secondary mouse button. Then drag to or click the name of the new toolbar in the toolbar QuickMenu that you want displayed.

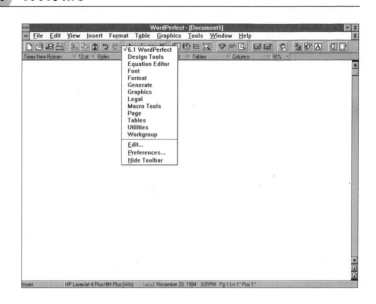

Moving the toolbar

You can move the toolbar by positioning the mouse pointer any-where on the toolbar where there are no buttons — on the bor-ders or in the extra gray space. As soon as the mouse pointer changes into a cupped hand, you can drag the toolbar to a new position.

If you release the mouse button when the outline of the toolbar is somewhere in the document window, the toolbar appears as a palette in its own window; you can resize this palette window and move it around the document window as you would resize and move any other window. To hide the toolbar, double-click the Control-menu button in the toolbar window. You can redisplay the toolbar by choosing Toolbar from the View menu.

You can also *dock* the toolbar along any one of the four borders of the program window. To do so, drag the outline (border) of the toolbar to one edge of the program window until the outline of the toolbar changes shape and conforms to the window's edge. Then release the mouse button.

Changing how the buttons appear

Normally, a toolbar displays only icons without displaying any text. To change the appearance of the buttons, follow these steps:

1. If the toolbar isn't already displayed on the screen, choose Toolbar from the View pull-down menu.

2. Click the toolbar with the secondary mouse button (the right button if you're a right-handed mouser or the left button if you're a left-handed mouser) and choose Preferences from the toolbar QuickMenu.

3. Choose Options in the Toolbar Preferences dialog box.

4. To display text on the buttons instead of a picture, choose the Text radio button under Appearance. To display both text and a picture on the buttons, choose the Picture and Text radio button.

5. To change the font of the text that appears on the buttons, choose a new font in the Font Face list box.

6. To change the size of the text on the buttons, choose a new size in the Font Size list box or enter a new size in the text box.

7. To change the location of the toolbar (without having to drag it around with the mouse), choose the Left, Top, Right, Bottom, or Palette radio button.

    When you choose any option other than Palette, the Maximum Number of Rows/Columns To Show option is available. With this option, you can enter in the text box the maximum number of rows (if the toolbar is at the top or bottom of the screen) or columns (if the bar is on the left or right) that you want WordPerfect for Windows to display.

8. By default, WordPerfect for Windows displays on the WordPerfect title bar the name of each button and a description of its function when you position the mouse pointer over it. If you don't want this display, deselect the Show QuickTips check box.

9. To add scroll buttons that enable you to scroll through the buttons of a toolbar containing too many buttons to be displayed in one screen, select the Show Scroll Bar option to put an X in its check box.

10. Choose OK or press Enter to close the Toolbar Options dialog box and then choose Close in the Toolbar Preferences dialog box.

To save room on your screen and still be able to distinguish the buttons easily, make sure that the Show QuickTips check box is selected; then just position the mouse pointer over a button to find out what it does.

Creating a custom toolbar

WordPerfect for Windows makes it easy to create your own toolbars. Follow these steps:

1. If the toolbar isn't already displayed on the screen, choose Toolbar from the View pull-down menu.

2. Click the toolbar with the secondary mouse button and then choose Preferences from the toolbar QuickMenu.

3. Choose Create in the Toolbar Preferences dialog box.

4. By default, WordPerfect for Windows stores the new toolbar with the current template. If you want to store the toolbar with whatever template is the default (Standard is the default unless you have changed it), first choose Template. Then choose the Default Template radio button in the Toolbar Location dialog box and choose OK or press Enter.

5. Type the name for your new toolbar in the New Toolbar Name text box. Then choose OK to open the Toolbar Editor, which shows the name of your new toolbar.

6. To add a button, choose the appropriate radio button under Add a Button To. (Activate a Feature adds a menu command, Play a Keyboard Script inserts text, Launch a Program starts a new program from WordPerfect for Windows, and Play a Macro executes a macro.)

   If you choose the Activate a Feature radio button, select the name of the pull-down menu (which includes the command that you want to add) in the Feature Categories list box. Then choose the particular command or feature in the Features list box and choose Add Button or press Enter.

   When you select a command in the Features list box, the program displays the icon and text used for that button with an explanation of what the button does. (This display is located under Add Button.) Then, instead of choosing Add Button or pressing Enter to insert the new button on the toolbar, you can click the feature in the list box and drag the hand-holding-a-button mouse pointer to the place on the toolbar where you want the new button to be added.

If you choose the Play a Keyboard Script radio button, choose the Type The Script This Button Plays option. Type the text that you want to insert in the document when you click the button and then choose Add Script or press Enter.

If you chose either the Launch a Program or the Play a Macro radio button, choose Select File, Add Macro, or Add Template Macro. In the Select File dialog box, choose the program file or macro file that you want the button to execute. Then press Enter to place the new button in the toolbar.

7. Repeat Step 6 until you have added all the buttons that you want to appear on the new toolbar.

8. To change the position of a button that you have added to the toolbar, press and drag the button to the place on the toolbar where you want it to appear and then release the mouse button.

9. To group two or more buttons together, you insert a space between a pair of buttons. To do so, click the Separator icon in the Toolbar Editor dialog box. When the mouse pointer changes into the hand-holding-a-separator, drag this pointer to the toolbar until it's between the buttons that you want to separate with a space and then release.

10. When you have finished adding and arranging buttons on the new toolbar, choose OK to close the Toolbar Editor dialog box and return to the Toolbar Preferences dialog box. Your new toolbar appears in the Available Toolbars list box.

11. To select the new toolbar, choose Select in the Toolbar Preferences dialog box. To leave current whatever toolbar was selected at the time you created your new toolbar, choose Close instead.

More stuff

Unlike feature bars (see the "Feature Bars" section), which have keyboard shortcuts so that you don't have to use a mouse to select buttons, buttons on a toolbar are accessible only by clicking the primary mouse button.

For more information about this command, see Chapter 2 of *WordPerfect For Windows For Dummies*.

Two Page View

Lets you see two pages of a document on the screen at one time.

Pull-down menu

More stuff

When you use two-page view in WordPerfect for Windows, you can edit the text and graphics as you would edit them on a normal-size page (if you can see the stuff that needs editing). You cannot, however, use the Zoom command to zoom in on a part of the two-page spread. To use the Zoom command, you must switch back to page view or draft view (see the sections "Draft View," "Page View," and "Zoom").

Typeover

Typeover is the typing mode opposite the default typing mode, which is Insert. In Typeover mode, the new characters you type on a line eat up the existing characters rather than push the existing characters to the right of the newly typed text (as is the case when you're using Insert mode).

More stuff

You can switch between Insert and Typeover modes by pressing Insert. WordPerfect for Windows always tells you when you have switched into Typeover mode by replacing Insert with Typeover on the Status bar.

For more information about this command, see Chapter 4 of *WordPerfect For Windows For Dummies.*

Undelete

Restores at the insertion point's current position any of the last three text deletions you made in your document.

Pull-down menu

![Screenshot of WordPerfect for Windows showing the Edit pull-down menu. Title bar reads "Restore one of your last three deletions - Ctrl+Shift+Z". The Edit menu shows: Undo Ctrl+Z, Redo Ctrl+Shift+R, Undo/Redo History..., Undelete... Ctrl+Shift+Z, Repeat..., Cut Ctrl+X, Copy Ctrl+C, Paste Ctrl+V, Append, Select, Paste Special..., Links..., Object..., Find and Replace... F2, Go To... Ctrl+G, Convert Case, Preferences...]

For keyboard kronies

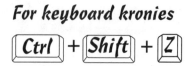

More stuff

When you press Ctrl+Shift+Z (or choose Undelete from the Edit menu), WordPerfect for Windows displays the Undelete dialog box. This box displays the last deletion you made as highlighted text at the insertion point's current position. To restore this text to the document, choose Restore. To see a previous deletion (up to the third one you made), choose Previous. To return to a deletion you have already seen, choose Next. When the text you want to restore appears, choose Restore. If the text never appears, choose Cancel or press Esc to close the Undelete dialog box.

For more information about this command, see Chapter 4 of *WordPerfect For Windows For Dummies*.

Underline

Underlines selected text in the document.

For keyboard kronies

| Ctrl | + | U |

For mouse maniacs

Click [U] on the WordPerfect 6.1 for Windows toolbar.

More stuff

You can underline text before or after you type it, just as you can with bold and italics (see the "Bold" section to get the general idea). To get rid of underlining in the text, open the Reveal Codes window and delete either the [Und> or the <Und] secret code that encloses the text.

For more information about this command, see Chapter 8 of *WordPerfect For Windows For Dummies*.

Undo

Restores the document to its previous state before you messed it up.

Pull-down menu

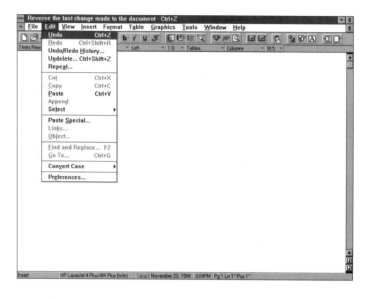

For keyboard kronies

To undo your last action press

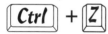

To redo your last action press

$Ctrl$ + $Shift$ + R

For mouse maniacs

To undo your last action, click on the WordPerfect 6.1 for Windows toolbar. To redo your last action, click instead.

More stuff

In WordPerfect 6.1 for Windows, you can undo (and redo) up to 300 of your past actions (wow!) — although WordPerfect for Windows is really only set up to undo the last ten actions when you start using the program. To increase the number of Undos and Redos allowed, choose Undo/Redo History on the Edit menu to open the Undo/Redo History dialog box. Then choose the Options button and enter the new number of Undos/Redos in the Number of Undo/Redo Items text box in the Undo/Redo Options dialog box.

To undo more than one action at a time, open the Undo/Redo History dialog box and then select the last item in the Undo list box that you want undone (WordPerfect for Windows will automatically select all items above the one you select) and click the Undo button. To redo more than one item, you perform the same sequence in the Redo list box and then choose the Redo button.

For more information about this command, see Chapter 2 of *WordPerfect For Windows For Dummies.*

Watermark

Inserts background text or graphics in a document that other text can be printed over and can still be read.

Pull-down menu

Creating a watermark

Creating a watermark is similar to creating a header or footer. (That's why they put Watermark right under Header/Footer on the Format menu.) To create a watermark, follow these steps:

1. Place the insertion point on the first page on which you want to have a watermark.

2. Choose Watermark from the Format menu to open the Watermark dialog box.

3. Choose Create to create Watermark A. (To create a second watermark, select Watermark B before you choose Create.)

   WordPerfect for Windows then opens a special Watermark window and displays the Watermark feature bar.

4. To add a graphics image to the watermark, choose Image on the Watermark feature bar and then choose a graphics file in the Insert Image dialog box. WordPerfect for Windows inserts the image as light gray in the document and displays the graphics box feature bar. Edit the light gray graphics image as you see fit and then choose Close, which closes the graphics box feature bar and returns to the Watermark feature bar.

5. To add text to your watermark, type the text in the Watermark window or open the document that contains the text. To do so, choose File on the Watermark features bar and then select the filename in the Insert File dialog box.

6. By default, if you add a watermark to your document, WordPerfect for Windows adds it to all pages in the document. To add the watermark to only the even or odd pages, choose Pages on the Watermark feature bar. Then choose the Odd Pages radio button or the Even Pages radio button.

7. When you finish entering and formatting the watermark text or adding the watermark graphics images, choose Close on the Watermark feature bar. The Watermark window and Watermark feature bar both close and you return to your document.

More stuff

Any watermark you add to a document is visible on the screen only when the program is in page view or two-page view. When you switch to draft view, the watermark image and text disappear from the screen.

 You can suppress the printing of a watermark on a specific page just as you can suppress a header or footer from printing (see the "Suppress" section for details).

Widow/Orphan (See "Keep Text Together")

Window

The Window commands let you switch between documents that are open in different windows and let you arrange all the open document windows on one screen. The arrangement of the windows can be overlapping or side-by-side. The Window pull-down menu also shows all the files that are currently open but that may not be active.

Pull-down menu

(Screenshot of WordPerfect window)

```
Switch to Document - Document1
 File  Edit  View  Insert  Format  Table  Graphics  Tools  Window  Help
                                                         Cascade
                                                         Tile Horizontal
 Times New Roman      12 pt   Styles      Left      1.0   Tile Vertical        91%

                                                        √1 Document1
```

```
Insert      HP LaserJet 4 Plus/4M Plus (Win)      November 20, 1994   3:05PM  Pg 1 Ln 1" Pos 1"
```

More stuff

To make another document window active, open the <u>W</u>indow menu and then type the underlined number given to the document window or click the number or filename with the mouse.

Choose <u>T</u>ile Horizontal, Tile <u>V</u>ertical, or <u>C</u>ascade from the <u>W</u>indow menu to arrange all the open windows. (You can have as many as nine windows open if your computer has enough memory.) <u>T</u>ile Horizontal places the windows side by side; Tile <u>V</u>ertical places the windows one on top of the other; <u>C</u>ascade places them one in front of the other with the title bars of each one showing.

For more information about this command, see Chapter 14 of *WordPerfect For Windows For Dummies*.

WordPerfect 6.0a Menu

Lets you switch the menu bar between the new 6.1 and old 6.0a menu arrangement.

For mouse maniacs

To change to WordPerfect for Windows 6.0a menus, click the menu bar with the secondary mouse button and choose <WPWin 6.0a Menu> on the menu bar QuickMenu. To change back to the new WordPerfect for Windows 6.1 menus, click the menu bar with the secondary mouse button and choose <WPWin 6.1 Menu> option on the menu bar QuickMenu.

WordPerfect Characters

Lets you insert special characters that are not available from the regular keyboard (such as weird foreign language and math and science symbols).

Pull-down menu

For keyboard kronies

$$\boxed{Ctrl} + \boxed{W}$$

More stuff

To insert a WordPerfect character into the text of your document or into a text box in a dialog box, position the insertion point where you want the character to appear. Then open the WordPerfect Characters dialog box (you must press Ctrl+W when you're in a dialog box). Choose the character set you want to use in the Character Set pop-up list and then select the character to use in the Characters list box. To insert the selected character and leave the WordPerfect Characters dialog box open, choose Insert (or double-click the character). To insert the selected character and also close the dialog box, choose Insert and Close.

Each WordPerfect character is assigned a set number plus a character number. This number is shown in the Number text box when you select a character in the Characters list box. If you already know the set number and character number for the character you want to use, select it by simply entering the two numbers in the Number text box and separate them with a comma.

Zoom

Lets you change the size of the screen display as you're running WordPerfect for Windows in draft view or page view.

Pull-down menu

For mouse maniacs

Click the Zoom button on the Power bar and drag to the Zoom command you want to use. Click [🔍] on the WordPerfect 6.1 for Windows toolbar to toggle between full page and the current zoom setting.

More stuff

Select the Margin Width radio button to have WordPerfect for Windows fill the document window with text from margin to margin and with minimal white space. Use Page Width to display the entire width of the document within the document window. Use Full Page to display the entire length of the document within the document window.

For more information about this command, see Chapter 20 of *WordPerfect For Windows For Dummies*.

Index

(continued)

(continued)

Notes

Notes

Here's a complete listing of IDG Books' ...For Dummies® titles

Title	Author	ISBN	Price
DATABASE			
Access 2 For Dummies®	by Scott Palmer	ISBN: 1-56884-090-X	$19.95 USA/$26.95 Canada
Access Programming For Dummies®	by Rob Krumm	ISBN: 1-56884-091-8	$19.95 USA/$26.95 Canada
Approach 3 For Windows® For Dummies®	by Doug Lowe	ISBN: 1-56884-233-3	$19.99 USA/$26.99 Canada
dBASE For DOS For Dummies®	by Scott Palmer & Michael Stabler	ISBN: 1-56884-188-4	$19.95 USA/$26.95 Canada
dBASE For Windows® For Dummies®	by Scott Palmer	ISBN: 1-56884-179-5	$19.95 USA/$26.95 Canada
dBASE 5 For Windows® Programming For Dummies®	by Ted Coombs & Jason Coombs	ISBN: 1-56884-215-5	$19.99 USA/$26.99 Canada
FoxPro 2.6 For Windows® For Dummies®	by John Kaufeld	ISBN: 1-56884-187-6	$19.95 USA/$26.95 Canada
Paradox 5 For Windows® For Dummies®	by John Kaufeld	ISBN: 1-56884-185-X	$19.95 USA/$26.95 Canada
DESKTOP PUBLISHING/ILLUSTRATION/GRAPHICS			
CorelDRAW! 5 For Dummies®	by Deke McClelland	ISBN: 1-56884-157-4	$19.95 USA/$26.95 Canada
CorelDRAW! For Dummies®	by Deke McClelland	ISBN: 1-56884-042-X	$19.95 USA/$26.95 Canada
Desktop Publishing & Design For Dummies®	by Roger C. Parker	ISBN: 1-56884-234-1	$19.99 USA/$26.99 Canada
Harvard Graphics 2 For Windows® For Dummies®	by Roger C. Parker	ISBN: 1-56884-092-6	$19.95 USA/$26.95 Canada
PageMaker 5 For Macs® For Dummies®	by Galen Gruman & Deke McClelland	ISBN: 1-56884-178-7	$19.95 USA/$26.95 Canada
PageMaker 5 For Windows® For Dummies®	by Deke McClelland & Galen Gruman	ISBN: 1-56884-160-4	$19.95 USA/$26.95 Canada
Photoshop 3 For Macs® For Dummies®	by Deke McClelland	ISBN: 1-56884-208-2	$19.95 USA/$26.95 Canada
QuarkXPress 3.3 For Dummies®	by Galen Gruman & Barbara Assadi	ISBN: 1-56884-217-1	$19.99 USA/$26.99 Canada
FINANCE/PERSONAL FINANCE/TEST TAKING REFERENCE			
Everyday Math For Dummies™	by Charles Seiter	ISBN: 1-56884-248-1	$14.99 USA/$22.99 Canada
Personal Finance For Dummies® For Canadians	by Eric Tyson & Tony Martin	ISBN: 1-56884-378-X	$18.99 USA/$24.99 Canada
QuickBooks 3 For Dummies®	by Stephen L. Nelson	ISBN: 1-56884-227-9	$19.99 USA/$26.99 Canada
Quicken 8 For DOS For Dummies® 2nd Edition	by Stephen L. Nelson	ISBN: 1-56884-210-4	$19.95 USA/$26.95 Canada
Quicken 5 For Macs® For Dummies®	by Stephen L. Nelson	ISBN: 1-56884-211-2	$19.95 USA/$26.95 Canada
Quicken 4 For Windows® For Dummies® 2nd Edition	by Stephen L. Nelson	ISBN: 1-56884-209-0	$19.95 USA/$26.95 Canada
Taxes For Dummies™ 1995 Edition	by Eric Tyson & David J. Silverman	ISBN: 1-56884-220-1	$14.95 USA/$20.99 Canada
The GMAT® For Dummies™	by Suzee Vlk, Series Editor	ISBN: 1-56884-376-3	$14.99 USA/$20.99 Canada
The GRE® For Dummies™	by Suzee Vlk, Series Editor	ISBN: 1-56884-375-5	$14.99 USA/$20.99 Canada
Time Management For Dummies™	by Jeffrey J. Mayer	ISBN: 1-56884-360-7	$16.99 USA/$22.99 Canada
TurboTax For Windows® For Dummies®	by Gail A. Helsel, CPA	ISBN: 1-56884-228-7	$19.99 USA/$26.99 Canada
GROUPWARE/INTEGRATED			
ClarisWorks For Macs® For Dummies®	by Frank Higgins	ISBN: 1-56884-363-1	$19.99 USA/$26.99 Canada
Lotus Notes For Dummies®	by Pat Freeland & Stephen Londergan	ISBN: 1-56884-212-0	$19.95 USA/$26.95 Canada
Microsoft® Office 4 For Windows® For Dummies®	by Roger C. Parker	ISBN: 1-56884-183-3	$19.95 USA/$26.95 Canada
Microsoft® Works 3 For Windows® For Dummies®	by David C. Kay	ISBN: 1-56884-214-7	$19.99 USA/$26.99 Canada
SmartSuite 3 For Dummies®	by Jan Weingarten & John Weingarten	ISBN: 1-56884-367-4	$19.99 USA/$26.99 Canada
INTERNET/COMMUNICATIONS/NETWORKING			
America Online® For Dummies® 2nd Edition	by John Kaufeld	ISBN: 1-56884-933-8	$19.99 USA/$26.99 Canada
CompuServe For Dummies® 2nd Edition	by Wallace Wang	ISBN: 1-56884-937-0	$19.99 USA/$26.99 Canada
Modems For Dummies® 2nd Edition	by Tina Rathbone	ISBN: 1-56884-223-6	$19.99 USA/$26.99 Canada
MORE Internet For Dummies®	by John R. Levine & Margaret Levine Young	ISBN: 1-56884-164-7	$19.95 USA/$26.95 Canada
MORE Modems & On-line Services For Dummies®	by Tina Rathbone	ISBN: 1-56884-365-8	$19.99 USA/$26.99 Canada
Mosaic For Dummies® Windows Edition	by David Angell & Brent Heslop	ISBN: 1-56884-242-2	$19.99 USA/$26.99 Canada
NetWare For Dummies® 2nd Edition	by Ed Tittel, Deni Connor & Earl Follis	ISBN: 1-56884-369-0	$19.99 USA/$26.99 Canada
Networking For Dummies®	by Doug Lowe	ISBN: 1-56884-079-9	$19.95 USA/$26.95 Canada
PROCOMM PLUS 2 For Windows® For Dummies®	by Wallace Wang	ISBN: 1-56884-219-8	$19.99 USA/$26.99 Canada
TCP/IP For Dummies®	by Marshall Wilensky & Candace Leiden	ISBN: 1-56884-241-4	$19.99 USA/$26.99 Canada

For scholastic requests & educational orders please call Educational Sales at 1. 800. 434. 2086

FOR MORE INFO OR TO ORDER, PLEASE CALL ▶ 800 762 2974

For volume discounts & special orders please call Tony Real, Special Sales, at 415. 655. 3048

The Internet For Macs® For Dummies® 2nd Edition	by Charles Seiter	ISBN: 1-56884-371-2	$19.99 USA/$26.99 Canada
The Internet For Macs® For Dummies® Starter Kit	by Charles Seiter	ISBN: 1-56884-244-9	$29.99 USA/$39.99 Canada
The Internet For Macs® For Dummies® Starter Kit Bestseller Edition	by Charles Seiter	ISBN: 1-56884-245-7	$39.99 USA/$54.99 Canada
The Internet For Windows® For Dummies® Starter Kit	by John R. Levine & Margaret Levine Young	ISBN: 1-56884-237-6	$34.99 USA/$44.99 Canada
The Internet For Windows® For Dummies® Starter Kit, Bestseller Edition	by John R. Levine & Margaret Levine Young	ISBN: 1-56884-246-5	$39.99 USA/$54.99 Canada

MACINTOSH

Mac® Programming For Dummies®	by Dan Parks Sydow	ISBN: 1-56884-173-6	$19.95 USA/$26.95 Canada
Macintosh® System 7.5 For Dummies®	by Bob LeVitus	ISBN: 1-56884-197-3	$19.95 USA/$26.95 Canada
MORE Macs® For Dummies®	by David Pogue	ISBN: 1-56884-087-X	$19.95 USA/$26.95 Canada
PageMaker 5 For Macs® For Dummies®	by Galen Gruman & Deke McClelland	ISBN: 1-56884-178-7	$19.95 USA/$26.95 Canada
QuarkXPress 3.3 For Dummies®	by Galen Gruman & Barbara Assadi	ISBN: 1-56884-217-1	$19.95 USA/$26.95 Canada
Upgrading and Fixing Macs® For Dummies®	by Kearney Rietmann & Frank Higgins	ISBN: 1-56884-189-2	$19.95 USA/$26.95 Canada

MULTIMEDIA

Multimedia & CD-ROMs For Dummies® 2nd Edition	by Andy Rathbone	ISBN: 1-56884-907-9	$19.99 USA/$26.99 Canada
Multimedia & CD-ROMs For Dummies® Interactive Multimedia Value Pack, 2nd Edition	by Andy Rathbone	ISBN: 1-56884-909-5	$29.99 USA/$39.99 Canada

OPERATING SYSTEMS:

DOS

MORE DOS For Dummies®	by Dan Gookin	ISBN: 1-56884-046-2	$19.95 USA/$26.95 Canada
OS/2® Warp For Dummies® 2nd Edition	by Andy Rathbone	ISBN: 1-56884-205-8	$19.99 USA/$26.99 Canada

UNIX

MORE UNIX® For Dummies®	by John R. Levine & Margaret Levine Young	ISBN: 1-56884-361-5	$19.99 USA/$26.99 Canada
UNIX® For Dummies®	by John R. Levine & Margaret Levine Young	ISBN: 1-878058-58-4	$19.95 USA/$26.95 Canada

WINDOWS

MORE Windows® For Dummies® 2nd Edition	by Andy Rathbone	ISBN: 1-56884-048-9	$19.95 USA/$26.95 Canada
Windows® 95 For Dummies®	by Andy Rathbone	ISBN: 1-56884-240-6	$19.99 USA/$26.99 Canada

PCS/HARDWARE

Illustrated Computer Dictionary For Dummies® 2nd Edition	by Dan Gookin & Wallace Wang	ISBN: 1-56884-218-X	$12.95 USA/$16.95 Canada
Upgrading and Fixing PCs For Dummies® 2nd Edition	by Andy Rathbone	ISBN: 1-56884-903-6	$19.99 USA/$26.99 Canada

PRESENTATION/AUTOCAD

AutoCAD For Dummies®	by Bud Smith	ISBN: 1-56884-191-4	$19.95 USA/$26.95 Canada
PowerPoint 4 For Windows® For Dummies®	by Doug Lowe	ISBN: 1-56884-161-2	$16.99 USA/$22.99 Canada

PROGRAMMING

Borland C++ For Dummies®	by Michael Hyman	ISBN: 1-56884-162-0	$19.95 USA/$26.95 Canada
C For Dummies® Volume 1	by Dan Gookin	ISBN: 1-878058-78-9	$19.95 USA/$26.95 Canada
C++ For Dummies®	by Stephen R. Davis	ISBN: 1-56884-163-9	$19.95 USA/$26.95 Canada
Delphi Programming For Dummies®	by Neil Rubenking	ISBN: 1-56884-200-7	$19.99 USA/$26.99 Canada
Mac® Programming For Dummies®	by Dan Parks Sydow	ISBN: 1-56884-173-6	$19.95 USA/$26.95 Canada
PowerBuilder 4 Programming For Dummies®	by Ted Coombs & Jason Coombs	ISBN: 1-56884-325-9	$19.99 USA/$26.99 Canada
QBasic Programming For Dummies®	by Douglas Hergert	ISBN: 1-56884-093-4	$19.95 USA/$26.95 Canada
Visual Basic 3 For Dummies®	by Wallace Wang	ISBN: 1-56884-076-4	$19.95 USA/$26.95 Canada
Visual Basic "X" For Dummies®	by Wallace Wang	ISBN: 1-56884-230-9	$19.99 USA/$26.99 Canada
Visual C++ 2 For Dummies®	by Michael Hyman & Bob Arnson	ISBN: 1-56884-328-3	$19.99 USA/$26.99 Canada
Windows® 95 Programming For Dummies®	by S. Randy Davis	ISBN: 1-56884-327-5	$19.99 USA/$26.99 Canada

SPREADSHEET

1-2-3 For Dummies®	by Greg Harvey	ISBN: 1-878058-60-6	$16.95 USA/$22.95 Canada
1-2-3 For Windows® 5 For Dummies® 2nd Edition	by John Walkenbach	ISBN: 1-56884-216-3	$16.95 USA/$22.95 Canada
Excel 5 For Macs® For Dummies®	by Greg Harvey	ISBN: 1-56884-186-8	$19.95 USA/$26.95 Canada
Excel For Dummies® 2nd Edition	by Greg Harvey	ISBN: 1-56884-050-0	$16.95 USA/$22.95 Canada
MORE 1-2-3 For DOS For Dummies®	by John Weingarten	ISBN: 1-56884-224-4	$19.99 USA/$26.99 Canada
MORE Excel 5 For Windows® For Dummies®	by Greg Harvey	ISBN: 1-56884-207-4	$19.95 USA/$26.95 Canada
Quattro Pro 6 For Windows® For Dummies®	by John Walkenbach	ISBN: 1-56884-174-4	$19.95 USA/$26.95 Canada
Quattro Pro For DOS For Dummies®	by John Walkenbach	ISBN: 1-56884-023-3	$16.95 USA/$22.95 Canada

UTILITIES

Norton Utilities 8 For Dummies®	by Beth Slick	ISBN: 1-56884-166-3	$19.95 USA/$26.95 Canada

VCRS/CAMCORDERS

VCRs & Camcorders For Dummies™	by Gordon McComb & Andy Rathbone	ISBN: 1-56884-229-5	$14.99 USA/$20.99 Canada

WORD PROCESSING

Ami Pro For Dummies®	by Jim Meade	ISBN: 1-56884-049-7	$19.95 USA/$26.95 Canada
MORE Word For Windows® 6 For Dummies®	by Doug Lowe	ISBN: 1-56884-165-5	$19.95 USA/$26.95 Canada
MORE WordPerfect® 6 For Windows® For Dummies®	by Margaret Levine Young & David C. Kay	ISBN: 1-56884-206-6	$19.95 USA/$26.95 Canada
MORE WordPerfect® 6 For DOS For Dummies®	by Wallace Wang, edited by Dan Gookin	ISBN: 1-56884-047-0	$19.95 USA/$26.95 Canada
Word 6 For Macs® For Dummies®	by Dan Gookin	ISBN: 1-56884-190-6	$19.95 USA/$26.95 Canada
Word For Windows® 6 For Dummies®	by Dan Gookin	ISBN: 1-56884-075-6	$16.95 USA/$22.95 Canada
Word For Windows® For Dummies®	by Dan Gookin & Ray Werner	ISBN: 1-878058-86-X	$16.95 USA/$22.95 Canada
WordPerfect® 6 For DOS For Dummies®	by Dan Gookin	ISBN: 1-878058-77-0	$16.95 USA/$22.95 Canada
WordPerfect® 6.1 For Windows® For Dummies® 2nd Edition	by Margaret Levine Young & David Kay	ISBN: 1-56884-243-0	$16.95 USA/$22.95 Canada
WordPerfect® For Dummies®	by Dan Gookin	ISBN: 1-878058-52-5	$16.95 USA/$22.95 Canada

For scholastic requests & educational orders please call Educational Sales at 1. 800. 434. 2086

FOR MORE INFO OR TO ORDER, PLEASE CALL ▶ 800. 762. 2974

For volume discounts & special orders please call Tony Real, Special Sales, at 415. 655. 3048

COMPUTER BOOK SERIES FROM IDG

For Dummies who want to program...

Delphi Programming For Dummies®
by Neil Rubenking

ISBN: 1-56884-200-7
$19.99 USA/$26.99 Canada

Access Programming For Dummies®
by Rob Krumm

ISBN: 1-56884-091-8
$19.95 USA/$26.95 Canada

TCP/IP For Dummies®
by Marshall Wilensky & Candace Leiden

ISBN: 1-56884-241-4
$19.99 USA/$26.99 Canada

HTML For Dummies®
by Ed Tittel & Carl de Cordova

ISBN: 1-56884-330-5
$29.99 USA/$39.99 Canada

Windows® 95 Programming For Dummies®
by S. Randy Davis

ISBN: 1-56884-327-5
$19.99 USA/$26.99 Canada

Mac® Programming For Dummies®
by Dan Parks Sydow

ISBN: 1-56884-173-6
$19.95 USA/$26.95 Canada

PowerBuilder 4 Programming For Dummies®
by Ted Coombs & Jason Coombs

ISBN: 1-56884-329-9
$19.99 USA/$26.99 Canada

Visual Basic 3 For Dummies®
by Wallace Wang

ISBN: 1-56884-076-4
$19.95 USA/$26.95 Canada

Covers version 3.

ISDN For Dummies®
by David Angell

ISBN: 1-56884-331-3
$19.99 USA/$26.99 Canada

Visual C++ "2" For Dummies®
by Michael Hyman & Bob Arnson

ISBN: 1-56884-328-3
$19.99 USA/$26.99 Canada

Borland C++ For Dummies®
by Michael Hyman

ISBN: 1-56884-162-0
$19.95 USA/$26.95 Canada

C For Dummies,® Volume I
by Dan Gookin

ISBN: 1-878058-78-9
$19.95 USA/$26.95 Canada

C++ For Dummies®
by Stephen R. Davis

ISBN: 1-56884-163-9
$19.95 USA/$26.95 Canada

QBasic Programming For Dummies®
by Douglas Hergert

ISBN: 1-56884-093-4
$19.95 USA/$26.95 Canada

dBase 5 For Windows® Programming For Dummies®
by Ted Coombs & Jason Coombs

ISBN: 1-56884-215-5
$19.99 USA/$26.99 Canada

For scholastic requests & educational orders please call Educational Sales at 1. 800. 434. 2086

FOR MORE INFO OR TO ORDER, PLEASE CALL ▸ 800 762 2974

For volume discounts & special orders please call Tony Real, Special Sales, at 415. 655. 3048

ORDER FORM

IDG BOOKS WORLDWIDE

Order Center: **(800) 762-2974** *(8 a.m.–6 p.m., EST, weekdays)*

10/09/95

Quantity	ISBN	Title	Price	Total

Shipping & Handling Charges

	Description	First book	Each additional book	Total
Domestic	Normal	$4.50	$1.50	$
	Two Day Air	$8.50	$2.50	$
	Overnight	$18.00	$3.00	$
International	Surface	$8.00	$8.00	$
	Airmail	$16.00	$16.00	$
	DHL Air	$17.00	$17.00	$

*For large quantities call for shipping & handling charges.
**Prices are subject to change without notice.

Ship to:

Name _____

Company _____

Address _____

City/State/Zip _____

Daytime Phone _____

Payment: ☐ Check to IDG Books Worldwide (US Funds Only)

☐ VISA ☐ MasterCard ☐ American Express

Card # _____ Expires _____

Signature _____

Subtotal _____

CA residents add
applicable sales tax _____

IN, MA, and MD
residents add
5% sales tax _____

IL residents add
6.25% sales tax _____

RI residents add
7% sales tax _____

TX residents add
8.25% sales tax _____

Shipping _____

Total _____

Please send this order form to:
IDG Books Worldwide, Inc.
7260 Shadeland Station, Suite 100
Indianapolis, IN 46256

Allow up to 3 weeks for delivery.
Thank you!

IDG BOOKS WORLDWIDE REGISTRATION CARD

RETURN THIS REGISTRATION CARD FOR FREE CATALOG

Title of this book: WP 6.1 For Windows For Dummies QR, 2E

My overall rating of this book: ❑ Very good [1] ❑ Good [2] ❑ Satisfactory [3] ❑ Fair [4] ❑ Poor [5]

How I first heard about this book:

❑ Found in bookstore; name: [6]

❑ Advertisement: [8]

❑ Word of mouth; heard about book from friend, co-worker, etc.: [10]

❑ Book review: [7]

❑ Catalog: [9]

❑ Other: [11]

What I liked most about this book:

What I would change, add, delete, etc., in future editions of this book:

Other comments:

Number of computer books I purchase in a year: ❑ 1 [12] ❑ 2-5 [13] ❑ 6-10 [14] ❑ More than 10 [15]

I would characterize my computer skills as: ❑ Beginner [16] ❑ Intermediate [17] ❑ Advanced [18] ❑ Professional [19]

I use ❑ DOS [20] ❑ Windows [21] ❑ OS/2 [22] ❑ Unix [23] ❑ Macintosh [24] ❑ Other: [25]_____
(please specify)

I would be interested in new books on the following subjects:
(please check all that apply, and use the spaces provided to identify specific software)

❑ Word processing: [26]

❑ Data bases: [28]

❑ File Utilities: [30]

❑ Networking: [32]

❑ Other: [34]

❑ Spreadsheets: [27]

❑ Desktop publishing: [29]

❑ Money management: [31]

❑ Programming languages: [33]

I use a PC at (please check all that apply): ❑ home [35] ❑ work [36] ❑ school [37] ❑ other: [38] _____

The disks I prefer to use are ❑ 5.25 [39] ❑ 3.5 [40] ❑ other: [41]_____

I have a CD ROM: ❑ yes [42] ❑ no [43]

I plan to buy or upgrade computer hardware this year: ❑ yes [44] ❑ no [45]

I plan to buy or upgrade computer software this year: ❑ yes [46] ❑ no [47]

Name: _____ Business title: [48] _____

Type of Business: [49]

Address (❑ home [50] ❑ work [51]/Company name: _____)

Street/Suite#

City [52]/State [53]/Zipcode [54]: _____ Country [55]

❑ **I liked this book!**
You may quote me by name in future IDG Books Worldwide promotional materials.

My daytime phone number is _____

IDG BOOKS

THE WORLD OF COMPUTER KNOWLEDGE

❑ **YES!**
Please keep me informed about IDG's World
of Computer Knowledge. Send me the latest
IDG Books catalog.

❏ YES!
Please keep me informed about IDG's World
of Computer Knowledge. Send me the latest
IDG Books catalog.

ORDER FORM

IDG BOOKS WORLDWIDE

Order Center: **(800) 762-2974** *(8 a.m.–6 p.m., EST, weekdays)*

Quantity	ISBN	Title	Price	Total
		.		

Shipping & Handling Charges

	Description	First book	Each additional book	Total
Domestic	Normal	$4.50	$1.50	$
	Two Day Air	$8.50	$2.50	$
	Overnight	$18.00	$3.00	$
International	Surface	$8.00	$8.00	$
	Airmail	$16.00	$16.00	$
	DHL Air	$17.00	$17.00	$

*For large quantities call for shipping & handling charges.
**Prices are subject to change without notice.

Ship to:

Name _____

Company _____

Address _____

City/State/Zip _____

Daytime Phone _____

Payment: ☐ Check to IDG Books Worldwide (US Funds Only)

☐ VISA ☐ MasterCard ☐ American Express

Card # _____ Expires _____

Signature _____

Subtotal _____

CA residents add
applicable sales tax _____

IN, MA, and MD
residents add
5% sales tax _____

IL residents add
6.25% sales tax _____

RI residents add
7% sales tax _____

TX residents add
8.25% sales tax _____

Shipping _____

Total _____

Please send this order form to:

IDG Books Worldwide, Inc.
7260 Shadeland Station, Suite 100
Indianapolis, IN 46256

Allow up to 3 weeks for delivery.
Thank you!

Outline

Creates outlines in your document just like your teacher had you make. When you create an outline, WordPerfect for Windows can automatically number the different levels for you. Then you can combine headings at various levels (as many as eight levels) with regular body text. You can also collapse the outline to hide all the body text so that only the outline headings are displayed, and later you can expand the outline to show everything again.

Pull-down menu

Creating an outline

You can use the outline feature to create formal outlines that would make your English teacher proud. When you create a formal outline, it can have as many as eight successive outline levels. WordPerfect for Windows automatically numbers and formats the entries in each level for you according to the outline style you choose.

To create an outline, just follow these steps:

1. Position the insertion point at the beginning of the line where you want the initial first-level heading of your outline to appear (usually on the first line after the one that contains the name of your outline).

2. Choose Outline from the Tools menu.

    WordPerfect for Windows switches to outline view, displays the Outline feature bar, and inserts the first outline number (1.). The program also indents the insertion point to the first tab stop. (The big, fat 1 you see in the left margin merely indicates that this is a first-level heading.)

3. Type the text of the initial first-level heading and then press Enter.

    WordPerfect for Windows inserts the second outline number (2.) and indents the insertion point so that you can enter the second first-level heading (indicated by the big, fat 1 in the left margin).

4. Type the second, first-level heading and press Enter. If you want to enter the initial second-level heading instead, press Tab to change the outline level (and change from 2. to a. and the big, fat 1 in the left margin to a big, fat 2). Then type the initial, second-level heading and press Enter.

5. WordPerfect for Windows enters the next number (or letter) in sequence for whatever outline level is current. Continue to enter all the headings you want at that level and terminate each one by pressing Enter. Whenever you want to enter a heading for the next-lower level, press Tab to move to the next outline level before entering the heading. Whenever you want to enter a heading at a higher level, press Shift+Tab until you have moved up the levels sufficiently before entering the heading. (Remember that the outline levels are indicated by the big, fat numbers in the left margin.)

6. When you finish entering the last heading for your outline, choose T on the Outline feature bar to convert the last outline number or letter to text (indicated by the big, fat T in the left margin). Then choose Close on the Outline feature bar to switch from outline view and close the Outline feature bar. (As a result, all the big, fat, outline-level numbers in the margin disappear, only to return when you next switch to outline view by choosing Outline from the Tools menu.)

Using the Outline feature bar

When you work with an outline, you can use the buttons on the Outline feature bar to make short work of your outline changes. Remember that WordPerfect for Windows displays the Outline feature bar as soon as you choose Outline from the Tools pull-down menu.

You can use the various buttons on the Outline feature bar to do neat stuff, like change a particular outline heading to the next or preceding outline level, convert regular document text to an outline heading, or convert an outline heading to regular text (with the nifty **T** button). You can also show only particular outline levels between 1 and 8 or None with the Show Outline Levels button or change the outline definition with the Options button.

Although WordPerfect for Windows automatically selects Paragraph, you can choose from several others in the drop-down list. Choose Outline if you want the outline style your teacher taught you: I., II., III., followed by A., B., C., followed by 1., 2., and 3., and so on down the line.

Page Borders (See "Borders")

Page Break

Inserts a *hard* (or manual) *page break* at the insertion point's position. Use this command whenever you want to place some text on a completely new page.

Pull-down menu

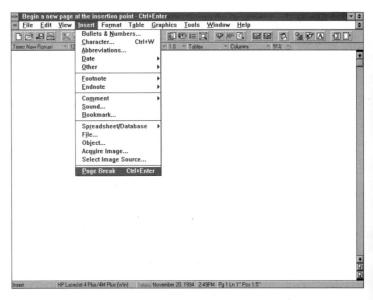

For keyboard kronies

$$\boxed{Ctrl} + \boxed{Enter}$$

More stuff

The secret code for a hard page break you insert in a document is [HPg]. The secret code for a soft page break that WordPerfect for Windows automatically inserts in a document is [SPg].

You can delete a hard page break by finding its secret code in the Reveal Codes window and zapping it. The only way to get rid of a soft page break is to change the format settings that affect the number of lines that fit on a page, such as the top and bottom margins, paper size, or line spacing.

Don't insert hard page breaks until after you have made all your editing changes in the document. Otherwise, when you print the document, you can easily end up with blank pages or pages that have just a little bit of text. Also, remember that WordPerfect for Windows provides a number of commands to keep certain text together on a page no matter how you edit the text.

You don't have to use hard page breaks to keep text from being separated if you utilize these commands (see the section "Keep Text Together").

For more information about this command, see Chapter 10 of *WordPerfect For Windows For Dummies*.

Page Numbering

Adds page numbers to your document, which WordPerfect for Windows automatically keeps up-to-date as you edit.

Pull-down menu

The Page Numbering dialog box

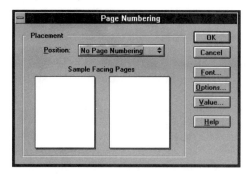

Option or Button	Function
Position	Lets you choose the position of the page numbers (which is then reflected in the Sample Facing Pages area in the Page Numbering dialog box).
Font	Lets you choose a new font, font size, and attribute for the page numbers in the Page Numbering Font dialog box.
Options	Lets you use the Format and Accompanying Text text box to add words to accompany the page number (such as *Page* so that you see Page 1 and Page 2 in the Sample Facing Pages). Lets you include a Secondary Number (such as Page 1, previously Page 2), Chapter Number (such as Chapter 1, Page 1), or Volume Number (such as Volume I, Page 1) in the page numbering by using Insert. Also lets you choose a new type of page numbering for the Page, Secondary, Chapter, and Volume numbers. You can choose Lowercase Letter, Uppercase Letter, Lowercase Roman, or Uppercase Roman.

Option or Button	*Function*
Value	Lets you change the initial page number for page, secondary, chapter, and volume numbers (either by entering a new number or increasing or decreasing the existing number by a certain amount). Also lets you insert the page, secondary page, chapter, or volume number in the document text at the insertion point.

More stuff

Be sure that the insertion point is somewhere on the first page that is to be numbered (page one if the whole document needs page numbers) before you select the Page Numbering command.

Rather than use the Page Numbering command to number the pages in your document, you can create a header or footer that displays the page number (see the section "Header/Footer").

For more information about this command, see Chapter 10 of *WordPerfect For Windows For Dummies.*

Displays your entire document and includes margins, headers, footers, page numbers, or footnotes — whatever appears in the top and bottom margin areas. (This is the default view in WordPerfect for Windows.)

Pull-down menu

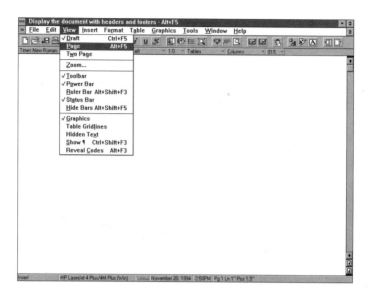

For keyboard kronies

More stuff

Switch to draft view when you want to maximize the amount of text on-screen and don't want to see stuff that's placed in the top and bottom margins.

For more information, refer to the sections "Draft View," "Two Page View," and "Zoom."

For more information about this command, see Chapter 10 of *WordPerfect For Windows For Dummies.*

Paper Size

Lets you choose a new paper size for all pages or particular pages in your document.

Pull-down menu

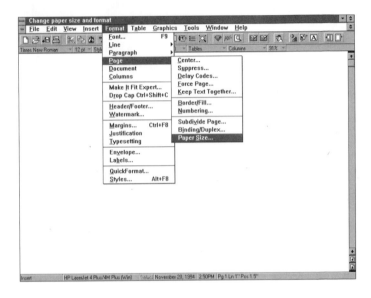

The Paper Size dialog box

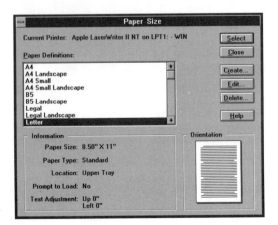

Option or Button	*Function*
<u>P</u>aper Definitions	Lets you choose the style of paper you want to use. When you choose a new style in the <u>P</u>aper Definitions list box, the program shows you the paper size, location, and orientation (among other things) at the bottom of the Paper Size dialog box.
<u>S</u>elect	Selects the paper you have highlighted in the <u>P</u>aper Definitions list box and returns you to the document.
C<u>r</u>eate	Lets you create a new paper definition for your printer in the Create Paper Size dialog box.
<u>E</u>dit	Lets you edit the paper definition that's highlighted in the <u>P</u>aper Definitions list box.
<u>D</u>elete	Lets you delete the paper definition that's highlighted in the Paper <u>D</u>efinitions list box.

More stuff

Before you choose a new paper size in the Paper Size dialog box, be sure that the insertion point is somewhere on the page that you're going to change. To change the size of a new page in the document, insert a hard page break by pressing Ctrl+Enter and then change the paper size.

Paragraph Borders (See "Borders")

Paragraph Format

Lets you indent the first line of a paragraph, change the spacing between paragraphs, and adjust the left and right margins of a paragraph (without adjusting the margins of the document).

Pull-down menu

Set paragraph formatting options

| File | Edit | View | Insert | **Format** | Table | Graphics | Tools | Window | Help |

Font...   F9
Line ▶
Paragraph   Format...
Page   Border/Fill...
Document
Columns   Indent   F7
    Hanging Indent Ctrl+F7
Make It Fit Expert...   Double Indent Ctrl+Shift+F7
Drop Cap Ctrl+Shift+C   Back Tab
Header/Footer...
Watermark...
Margins... Ctrl+F8
Justification ▶
Typesetting ▶
Envelope...
Labels...
QuickFormat...
Styles... Alt+F8

Times New Roman   12 pt   Style   91%

Insert   HP LaserJet 4 Plus/4M Plus (Win)   Select November 20, 1994   2:50PM   Pg 1 Ln 1" Pos 1.5"

For mouse maniacs

Click 📖 on the WordPerfect 6.1 for Windows toolbar.

The Paragraph Format dialog box

Paragraph Format

First Line Indent: `0"`

Spacing Between Paragraphs: `1`

Paragraph Adjustments

Left Margin Adjustment: `0"`

Right Margin Adjustment: `0"`

OK

Cancel

Clear All

Help

Option or Button	Function
First Line Indent	Lets you specify how far to indent only the first line of each paragraph.
Spacing Between Paragraphs	Lets you adjust the spacing between paragraphs (one line by default).
Left Margin Adjustment	Lets you indent the left edge of each paragraph without changing the left margin for the document.
Right Margin Adjustment	Lets you indent the right edge of each paragraph without changing the right margin for the document.
Clear All	Clears all changes made in the Paragraph Format dialog box and returns you to the default settings.

More stuff

Be sure that the insertion point is in the first paragraph you want to adjust before you change the settings in the Paragraph Format dialog box.

If you reach a paragraph in the document in which you want to return to normal formatting, place the insertion point in that paragraph. Then open the Paragraph Format dialog box and choose Clear All.

For more information about this command, see Chapter 9 of *WordPerfect For Windows For Dummies*.

Power Bar

A bar that appears at the top of the program window with buttons on it that you mouse maniacs can use to do common things, such as open, save, or print a document.

Pull-down menu

The buttons on the Power bar

By default, the Power bar contains the following buttons:

Button	Function
Font Face	Lets you change the font used in the document text (this button shows the current font, as in Times New Roman).
Font Size	Lets you change the size of the font used in the document text (this button shows the current font size, as in 12 pt).
Styles	Lets you select a style for your document (this button shows the name of the current style, or Styles when none is selected).

(continued)

Button	Function
Justification	Lets you change the justification of the text in the document (this button shows the current justification, as in Left for left justification). See "Justification" for more on changing the text alignment.
Line Spacing	Lets you change the line spacing used in the document text (this button shows the current line spacing, as in 1.0 for single spacing).
Tables	Lets you create a table in the document by dragging through a miniature spreadsheet that appears when you double-click its button (this button always shows Tables).
Columns	Lets you set up to five newspaper columns in your document (this button shows the current number of newspaper columns, or Columns when newspaper columns are turned off). See "Columns" for more on setting up and using columns in WordPerfect for Windows.
Zoom	Lets you change magnification of the document text (this button shows the current magnification, as in 100% for actual size).

QuickMenus

To modify the buttons on the Power bar, click the Power bar with the secondary mouse button (the right button if you're a right-handed mouser, or the left button if you're a left-handed mouser) and choose Edit from the QuickMenu. Choose Hide Power Bar from the QuickMenu when you want the Power bar to go away.

More stuff

To find out what a particular button does, position the mouse pointer on the button. WordPerfect for Windows then displays the button's function on the title bar of the program window.

For more information about this command, see Chapter 2 of *WordPerfect For Windows For Dummies*.

Print

Prints all or part of the document located in the current document editing window.

Pull-down menu

For keyboard kronies

$$\boxed{Ctrl} + \boxed{p}$$

For mouse maniacs

Click 🖳 on the WordPerfect 6.1 for Windows toolbar.

The Print dialog box

```
┌──────────────────────────────────────────────────────────┐
│ ▄                          Print                          │
│ ┌────────────────────────────────────────┐  ┌──────────┐ │
│ │ Current Printer                        │  │  Print   │ │
│ │ Apple LaserWriter II NT on LPT1: - WIN │  └──────────┘ │
│ │                              [Select...] │  ┌──────────┐ │
│ │                                        │  │  Close   │ │
│ └────────────────────────────────────────┘  └──────────┘ │
│ ┌─Print Selection─┐ ┌─Copies───────────┐    ┌──────────┐ │
│ │                 │ │                  │    │Initialize│ │
│ │ ◉ Full Document │ │ Number of Copies: [1] ⬍  │      │ │
│ │                 │ │                  │    │ Options..│ │
│ │ ○ Current Page  │ │ Generated By: [WordPerfect ⬍]│   │ │
│ │                 │ │                  │    │ Control  │ │
│ │ ○ Multiple Pages│ └──────────────────┘    └──────────┘ │
│ │                 │ ┌─Document Settings┐    ┌──────────┐ │
│ │ ○ Selected Text │ │                  │    │  Help    │ │
│ │                 │ │ Print Quality: [High      ⬍]│     │ │
│ │ ○ Document Summary│ │                │    └──────────┘ │
│ │                 │ │ Print Color:  [Black      ⬍]│      │ │
│ │ ○ Document on Disk│ │ □ Do Not Print Graphics │        │ │
│ └─────────────────┘ └──────────────────┘              │ │
└──────────────────────────────────────────────────────────┘
```

Option or Button	Function
Select	Lets you use the Select Printer dialog box to choose a new printer to use (either a printer you installed with Windows or a WordPerfect printer you installed when you installed the program).
Print Selection	Lets you select which section of the document to print. You can choose Full Document (the default), Current Page, Multiple Pages, Selected Text, Document Summary, or Document on Disk.
Copies	Lets you specify the number of copies to print, using the Number of Copies text box. The Generated By pop-up list lets you determine whether WordPerfect generates the copies (they're all collated) or your Printer generates them (you collate them yourself).

Option or Button	*Function*
Document Settings	Lets you change the Print Quality (normally High) and choose a new Print Color (if you're using a color printer). Also lets you omit the printing of graphics by putting an X in the Do Not Print Graphics check box. This option is useful when you want a quick printout and want only to proof the document text.
Initialize	Lets you initialize the printer if you want to clear the printer's memory before printing your document.
Options	Lets you specify some pretty fancy formatting and output printing options. These options include Print in Reverse Order (Back to Front); Print Odd/Even Pages, which prints only the odd or even pages in the document; specifying which output bin to use; and arranging the pages in the chosen bin.
Control	Lets you control the print queue when you print your document on a networked printer.

Printing particular pages

Many times, you want to print only a part of your document. When you select the Multiple Pages radio button in the Print dialog box and choose Print, WordPerfect for Windows displays the Multiple Pages dialog box. This is where you can specify which pages to print.

When you specify the range of pages in this dialog box (secondary pages, chapters, or volumes), be sure to enter the page numbers in numerical order. To specify a range of pages, use a hyphen as follows:

--10	Print from the beginning to page 10
10--	Print from page 10 to the last page
3--10	Print from page 3 to page 10

To specify individual pages, put a comma between the page numbers, as in the following example:

`4,10,23`

Only pages 4, 10, and 23 are then printed. You can also combine ranges and individual pages, as in the following example:

`3-7,9,25`

Using these commands, only the range of pages 3 through 7 and pages 9 and 23 are printed.

More stuff

When you select P̲rint to begin a print job, WordPerfect for Windows sends the print job to the WP Print Process program. This program in turn ships it off to the Windows Print Manager. If you want to cancel the printing, you must switch to the WP Print Process or Print Manager window and cancel the printing from there. To switch to either program, click the Control-menu button in the upper-left corner of the WordPerfect for Windows program window and choose S̲witch To (or press Ctrl+Esc). Then choose WP Print Process or Print Manager in the Task List dialog box.

For more information about this command, see Chapter 13 of *WordPerfect For Windows For Dummies.*

QuickCorrect

Lets you designate the typos that you routinely make and tell WordPerfect which corrections it should automatically undertake the moment your erring fingers make these boo-boos.

Pull-down menu

![Screenshot of pull-down menu with Tools menu open showing Spell Check, Thesaurus, Grammatik, QuickCorrect, Language, Macro, Template Macro, Merge, Sort, Outline, Hypertext, List, Index, Cross-Reference, Table of Contents, Table of Authorities, Generate]

For keyboard kronies

$$\boxed{Ctrl} + \boxed{Shift} + \boxed{F1}$$

The QuickCorrect dialog box

![QuickCorrect dialog box showing Replace and With columns with entries like (c)/©, 1/2/½, acomodate/accommodate, acsesory/accessory, adn/and, adress/address, allready/already, alot/a lot, antartic/antarctic, aparent/apparent, april/April, aquaintance/acquaintance, artic/arctic, asma/asthma. Buttons: Add Entry, Delete Entry, Options, Close, Help. Checkbox: Replace Words as You Type]

Option or Button	Function
Replace	Type the incorrect spelling that you invariably enter in your document in this text box.
With	In this text box, type the correct (make sure that it's correct) spelling that you want WordPerfect to use whenever you type the incorrect spelling you just entered in the Replace text box.
Add Entry	Click this button to add your new QuickCorrect entry to the list.
Delete Entry	Click this button to remove the selected QuickCorrect entry from its list box.
Options	Click this button to change the sentence and end of sentence QuickCorrect options (such as automatically capitalizing the first letter of a sentence, correcting two capital letters at the start of a word, and reducing double spaces between words to single spaces).
Replace Words as You Type	Keep this check box checked if you want WordPerfect to make corrections as soon as you make the typo. If you deselect this check box, the program will not make your corrections until you spell check the part of the document containing the boo-boo (see "Spell Check" for details on spell checking a document).

QuickFormat

Copies the formatting used in the current paragraph and then allows you to apply this formatting to other selections of text in the document.

Pull-down menu

For mouse maniacs

Click [icon] on the WordPerfect 6.1 for Windows toolbar.

QuickMenus

Move the insertion point to somewhere in the paragraph that contains the formatting you want to use. Click again, this time with the secondary mouse button (the right button if you're a right-handed mouser, or the left button if you're a left-handed mouser), and choose QuickFormat from the QuickMenu.

Formatting: As easy as selecting text

To use the QuickFormat feature, position the insertion point in the paragraph whose formatting you want to use elsewhere in the document. Then choose QuickFormat from the Format pull-down menu or click anywhere in the text with the secondary mouse button and choose QuickFormat from the QuickMenu.

WordPerfect for Windows opens the QuickFormat dialog box, where you specify the QuickFormat options you want to use. By default, the program copies the fonts, attributes, and styles used in the original paragraph. If you want to use only the fonts and attributes found in the current paragraph text, choose the Fonts and Attributes radio button. If you want to use only the styles currently in effect, choose the Characters radio button.

When you choose OK or press Enter to close the QuickFormat dialog box, the mouse pointer changes to an I-beam with a paint roller beside it. Use this roller to select all the text you want formatted with the fonts, attributes, and styles found in the original paragraph. As soon as you release the mouse button after selecting the text, the text immediately takes on the font, attribute, and paragraph style formatting used in the original selected paragraph.

More stuff

When you no longer want to use the pointer to "quick" format text, you can change the pointer back to normal. Simply choose QuickFormat from the Format pull-down menu or the text QuickMenu.

QuickMark (see "Bookmark")

QuickMenu

Lets you select commands from a limited pull-down menu that appears when you click an object (such as text or a graphics box) with the secondary mouse button (the right mouse button for right-handers, and the left mouse button for lefties).

More stuff

In WordPerfect for Windows, you can find QuickMenus attached to each of the following screen objects:

- Left margin area of the document (see the section "Select (Text)")
- Top and bottom area of the document (see the section "Header/Footer")
- Menu bar

- Toolbar (see the "Toolbars" section)
- Power bar (see the "Power Bar" section)
- Scroll bars
- Status bar
- Feature bars (see the "Feature Bar" section)
- Document area and document text
- Graphics boxes (see the "Graphics Boxes" section)
- Table cells (see the "Tables" section)

Redline/Strikeout (See "Font")

Repeat

Repeats a keystroke or action, such as moving the insertion point or deleting a character, a set number of times.

Pull-down menu

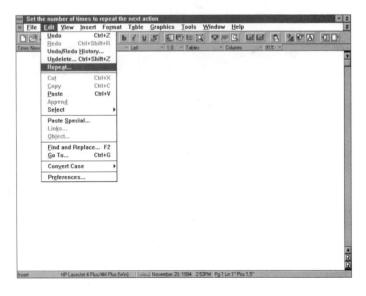

Could you repeat that, please?

Repeat is one of those WordPerfect for Windows features that seems really neat when you first hear about it but is too often overlooked when you're actually editing. WordPerfect for Windows originally added this feature to make it easy to insert a string of characters into your document, such as ———— or ********.

To repeat a character, choose Repeat from the Edit menu and choose OK or press Enter to close the Repeat dialog box. Then type the single character or perform the action you want to repeat.

By default, WordPerfect for Windows repeats eight times the character you type. If you want more or fewer repetitions, type a new number in the Number of Times to Repeat Next Action text box before you choose OK or press Enter. Then type the character to be repeated.

More stuff

You can use the Repeat feature to repeat certain keystrokes and to type characters. You can delete the next eight characters from the insertion point by pressing Delete after opening the Repeat dialog box, for example. Or you can move the insertion point in your document eight characters to the right by pressing the → key. You can move eight pages up in the document by opening the Repeat dialog box and then pressing PgUp.

Reveal Codes

Opens the Reveal Codes window at the bottom of the document editing window. As you edit and format your text, you can view as well as edit all those wacky secret codes WordPerfect for Windows insists on putting in your document.

Pull-down menu

For keyboard kronies

$$\boxed{Alt} + \boxed{F3}$$

For mouse maniacs

To open the Reveal Codes window with the mouse, position the mouse pointer on either of the two solid, black bars that appear at the very top or bottom of the vertical scroll bar. When the pointer becomes a double-headed arrow pointing up and down, drag the mouse up or down until the border between the regular document window and the Reveal Codes window is where you want it. Then release the mouse button.

To close the Reveal Codes window with the mouse, position the mouse pointer somewhere on the border between the regular document window and the Reveal Codes window. When the pointer becomes an arrow pointing up and down, drag the border all the way up or down until you reach the Power bar or Status bar. Then release the mouse button.

QuickMenus

To modify the appearance of the codes in the Reveal Codes window, click anywhere in the Reveal Codes window with the secondary mouse button (the right mouse button for right-handers and the left mouse button for lefties). Then choose Pr<u>e</u>ferences from the QuickMenu. Choose <u>H</u>ide Reveal Codes from the QuickMenu when you want the Reveal Codes window to go away.

Using Reveal Codes

Reveal Codes gives you a behind-the-scenes look at the placement of all the formatting codes that tell your printer how to produce special effects in your document. You can see codes that define new margin settings, define tabs, center and bold lines of text, set larger font sizes for titles and headings, create paragraph borders around your footer text, and so on.

This information is of absolutely no concern to a normal human being unless, of course, something is wrong with the format of a document and you can't figure how to fix it by using the normal editing window. That's the time when you have to "get under the hood," so to speak, by opening the Reveal Codes window. Then you can edit with all those little secret codes in full view.

When you're editing with the Reveal Codes window open, use the regular document editing window above it to find your general place in the document. Then concentrate on what's happening in the Reveal Codes window to make your changes. You mouse maniacs can use the mouse to reposition the Reveal Codes cursor in the Reveal Codes window by simply clicking the mouse pointer where you want it to be. (It's not really an insertion point in this window because it appears as a red block.)

To delete a code, position the Reveal Codes cursor either directly in front of or behind the code. If the cursor is in front of the code, press Delete to get rid of it. If the cursor is behind the code, press Backspace to back over the code and delete it. If you're using the mouse, you can remove a code by selecting it and then dragging it until the pointer is outside the Reveal Codes window. Then you can release the mouse button.

More stuff

You can change the normal size of the codes in addition to other appearance options. To do so, choose Preferences from the Edit pull-down menu and double-click the Display icon. Then choose the Reveal Codes radio button in the Display Preferences dialog box. You can change all the settings you want, including the font and font size of the text or any of the settings in the Options area that control the appearance of the codes in the Reveal Codes window. You can also change the size of the Reveal Codes window.

For more information about this command, see Chapter 11 of *WordPerfect For Windows For Dummies*.

Ruler Bar

The ruler bar shows the current settings of the tabs and the left and right margins at the insertion point. You can manipulate the tab and margin icons to change these settings.

Pull-down menu

Show the Ruler Bar - Alt+Shift+F3

| File | Edit | View | Insert | Format | Table | Graphics | Tools | Window | Help |

√ Draft   Ctrl+F5
Page   Alt+F5
Two Page

Zoom...

√ Toolbar
√ Power Bar
Ruler Bar Alt+Shift+F3
√ Status Bar
Hide Bars Alt+Shift+F5

√ Graphics
Table Gridlines
Hidden Text
Show ¶ Ctrl+Shift+F3
Reveal Codes Alt+F3

Insert   HP LaserJet 4 Plus/4M Plus (Win)   Select November 20, 1994 2:54PM Pg 1 Ln 1" Pos 1.5"

For keyboard kronies

$\boxed{Alt} + \boxed{Shift} + \boxed{F3}$

For mouse maniacs

```
WordPerfect - [Document1 - unmodified]
File  Edit  View  Insert  Format  Table  Graphics  Tools  Window  Help
```

Double-click the tab ruler on the ruler bar to bring up the Display Preferences dialog box. Double-click a tab icon on the tab ruler to display the Tab Set dialog box. Double-click the left- or right-margin icon or the white space between them above the tab ruler to display the Margins dialog box. Double-click the triangles next to the left- and right-margin icons (representing the paragraph margins) to display the Paragraph Format dialog box.

To change the left or right margin settings, drag the left- or right-margin icon above the tab ruler. To change the left indent of your paragraphs, drag the bottom triangle that points left. (Both the top and bottom triangles move together.) To change the right indent of the paragraphs, drag the bottom triangle that points right so that it's next to the right-margin icon. To change the indent of only the first line of the paragraphs, drag just the top triangle that points left.

To change a tab setting, drag the tab icon to a new position on the tab ruler. To remove a tab setting, drag the tab icon off the tab ruler. To add a new tab, select the type of tab (Left, Center, Right, Decimal, ...Left, ...Center, ...Right, or ...Decimal) on the Ruler Bar QuickMenu and then click the place on the tab ruler where you want this tab to be added.

QuickMenus

You can use the QuickMenu associated with the ruler bar to change the tab settings, change that paragraph format, adjust margins, set columns, or create tables. You can also use the QuickMenu to hide the ruler bar or change the ruler bar display preferences. To open the QuickMenu, click anywhere in the area of the ruler bar, which is marked by the left- and right-margin icons above the tab ruler.

You can use the QuickMenu associated with each tab to select a
new type of tab, clear all tabs from the ruler, change the tab settings in the Tab Set dialog box, or hide the ruler bar or change the
ruler bar display preferences. To open this QuickMenu, click anywhere on a tab icon with the secondary mouse button (the right
mouse button for right-handers, and the left mouse button for lefties).

More stuff

You can also change the margin settings by using the Margins dialog box and your tab settings by using the Tab Set dialog box.
(See the sections "Margins" and "Tab Set" for more information.)

For more information about this command, see Chapter 2 of
WordPerfect For Windows For Dummies.

Save

Lets you save your changes to a document on disk so that you
have a copy of the document for future use. The first time you
save, you must give the document a new filename. After that, you
can use this command to save your changes to that file as you
continue to work.

Pull-down menu

For keyboard kronies

For mouse maniacs

Click 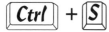 on the WordPerfect 6.1 for Windows toolbar to save your document.

Saving a file for the first time

To save a file for the first time, you have to go through the whole rigmarole described in this section. After that, however, you only have to choose Save from the File menu to save your changes. (WordPerfect for Windows doesn't bother with filenames, passwords, and that kind of stuff.) To initially save your file, follow these steps:

1. Choose Save from the File menu or press Ctrl+S; the program displays the Save As dialog box.

2. By using the Drives drop-down list box, the QuickList, or the Directories list box, select the drive and directory in which you want the file to be saved.

3. Type the name for your new file in the Filename text box. The main filename can be as long as eight characters and the (optional) filename extension can be as long as three characters. The extension is separated from the main filename with a period.

4. To assign a password to your file, choose the Password Protect option to put an X in its check box.

5. Choose OK or press Enter to save the document.

6. If you checked the Password Protect box, the Password dialog box appears. Type the password just as you want it recorded and differentiate uppercase from lowercase letters. (Notice that WordPerfect for Windows masks each character you type.) Choose OK or press Enter. You must then retype the password exactly as you originally typed it and again choose OK or press Enter.

   If you mess up and type the password a little differently the second time, WordPerfect for Windows displays a dialog box which lets you know that the passwords don't match and lets you try again after choosing OK or pressing Enter to clear the Alert dialog box.

More stuff

Spare yourself lots of heartbreak and wasted time by saving your documents often. Save every time you are interrupted (by the telephone, your boss, or whatever) and save whenever you have made more changes to the document than you would ever want to have to redo.

Save As

Lets you change the name or location of your WordPerfect for Windows document. You can even save your document in a different file format. This way, coworkers less fortunate than you who have to use some other word processor can have access to your document.

Pull-down menu

For keyboard kronies

F3

The Save As dialog box

```
┌─────────────────────────────────────────────────────────┐
│ ═                           Save As                      │
│                                                          │
│ Filename:          c:\office\wpwin\wpdocs    ┌─────────┐ │
│ ┌─────────────┐ ±                            │   OK    │ │
│ │ *.*         │     QuickList:               └─────────┘ │
│ └─────────────┘     Documents                ┌─────────┐ │
│ ┌─────────────┐     Graphics Directory       │ Cancel  │ │
│ │             │     Macro Directory          └─────────┘ │
│ │             │     Printer Directory        ┌─────────┐ │
│ │             │     Template Directory       │ View... │ │
│ │             │                              └─────────┘ │
│ │             │     Directories:             ┌──────────┐│
│ │             │     ┌──────────────┐         │QuickFinder││
│ │             │     │ 🗀 c:\        │         └──────────┘│
│ │             │     │   🗀 office   │         ┌─────────┐ │
│ │             │     │     🗀 wpwin  │         │File Options ▾│
│ │             │     │       🗀 wpdocs│        └─────────┘ │
│ │             │     └──────────────┘         ┌─────────┐ │
│ │             │                              │QuickList ▾│
│ │             │                              └─────────┘ │
│ │             │                              ┌─────────┐ │
│ │             │                              │ Setup...│ │
│ │             │                              └─────────┘ │
│ │             │                              ┌─────────┐ │
│ │             │                              │Network ▾│ │
│ Total Files: 0     Drives:  690,464 KB Free  └─────────┘ │
│ Total Bytes: 0     ┌──────────────┐ ±        ┌─────────┐ │
│ Sort: Filename Ascending│ 💾 c:    │         │  Help   │ │
│ Save File as Type: │WordPerfect 6.0/6.1 [*.wpd;*.wpt;*.doc ±│ └─────────┘ │
│                              ☐ Password Protect          │
└─────────────────────────────────────────────────────────┘
```

Option	Function
Filename	Lets you change the filename of your document. To make a copy under the same filename but in a new directory, just type a new pathname and leave the filename unchanged.
QuickList	Lets you change to the directory in which the document is saved by selecting the alias that you gave the directory name in the QuickList list box.
Directories	Lets you change the directory, if you want to save the file in a directory other than the current one.
Drives	Lets you change the drive if you want to save the file on a disk in a different drive.

Option	*Function*
Save File as <u>T</u>ype	Lets you save the document in another file format. (WordPerfect 6.1 For Windows supports a bunch.) Just select the new format type in the drop-down list.
<u>P</u>assword Protect	Lets you password-protect your file. Don't mess with a password unless you are really sure that you won't forget it. (It's a good idea to write down any passwords and store them in a secure place. This way, coworkers can get into your files if you suddenly decide to chuck it all and live in Tahiti.)

Button	*Function*
Vie<u>w</u>	Lets you preview in a separate window the contents of the file that is selected in the File<u>n</u>ame list box.
Quick<u>F</u>inder	Lets you locate a particular document by searching indexed directories for a file created between a range of dates or containing specific text or word patterns.
File <u>O</u>ptions	Lets you perform tasks to the files selected in the File<u>n</u>ame list box, such as copying, moving, renaming, deleting, or printing.
Quick<u>L</u>ist	Lets you assign a QuickList alias to a particular directory.
<u>S</u>etup	Lets you change the way files are listed in the File<u>n</u>ame list box and lets you designate how much file information you want to include in the list.
Networ<u>k</u>	Lets you change network settings if you're using WordPerfect 6.1 for Windows on a Local Area Network. This is not something you want to undertake unless you've discussed what settings need tweaking with some sort of techie expert or network guru in your organization.

More stuff

Use <u>S</u>ave from the <u>F</u>ile menu when you want to save editing and formatting changes to the document and update the file. Use Save <u>A</u>s to save the document with a new filename or in a new directory, in another file format for use with another word processor, or if someone convinces you that you need to add a password to the document.

For more information about this command, see Chapter 15 of *WordPerfect For Windows For Dummies.*

Search and Replace (See "Find and Replace")

Select (Text)

Marks a section of text so that you can do all sorts of neat things to it, such as cut and paste it, spell-check it, print it, or even get rid of it.

Pull-down menu

Select the entire document		

File <u>E</u>dit <u>V</u>iew Insert Fo<u>r</u>mat T<u>a</u>ble <u>G</u>raphics <u>T</u>ools <u>W</u>indow <u>H</u>elp

<u>U</u>ndo   Ctrl+Z
<u>R</u>edo   Ctrl+Shift+R
Undo/Redo <u>H</u>istory...
U<u>n</u>delete... Ctrl+Shift+Z
Rep<u>e</u>at...

Cu<u>t</u>   Ctrl+X
<u>C</u>opy   Ctrl+C
<u>P</u>aste   Ctrl+V
Appen<u>d</u>
<u>S</u>elect

Paste <u>S</u>pecial...
Lin<u>k</u>s...
<u>O</u>bject...

<u>F</u>ind and Replace... F2
<u>G</u>o To...   Ctrl+G

Con<u>v</u>ert Case   ▶

P<u>r</u>eferences...

Sentence
P<u>a</u>ragraph
P<u>a</u>ge
<u>A</u>ll

Tabular <u>C</u>olumn
<u>R</u>ectangle

Insert   HP LaserJet 4 Plus/4M Plus [Win]   Select   November 20, 1994   2:55PM   Pg 1 Ln 1" Pos 1.5"

For keyboard kronies

QuickMenus

Click the secondary mouse pointer (the right mouse button for right-handers, and the left mouse button for lefties) in the left margin area of the document. Then choose one of the following: Select <u>S</u>entence to select the current sentence; Select <u>P</u>aragraph to select the current paragraph; Select P<u>a</u>ge to select the current page; or Select A<u>l</u>l to select the entire document.

For mouse maniacs

Position the mouse pointer in front of the first character of text that is to be highlighted and drag the pointer through the entire block of text. To select the current word, double-click somewhere in the word. To select the current paragraph, triple-click somewhere in the paragraph. To select a block of text, click the insertion point in front of the first character, press and hold Shift, and then click the last character. WordPerfect for Windows highlights all the text in between.

Marking selections keyboard-style

To mark a selection with the keyboard, follow these steps:

1. Position the insertion point in front of the first character to be included in the selection.

2. Press F8 or press and hold Shift. The Select indicator on the Status bar becomes activated.

3. Use the insertion-point movement keys to extend the selection (see the section "Insertion Point" for details). WordPerfect for Windows highlights all the text you cover as you move the insertion point.

Other slick ways to extend a block

WordPerfect for Windows offers all sorts of fast ways to extend a selected block after you have turned on blocking. This list shows a few shortcuts you might want to try:

• Press Ctrl+→ to extend the block to the next word to the right or Ctrl+←to extend the block to the next word to the left.

- Press ↑ to extend the block up one line. Press ↓ to extend the block down one line.

- Press Ctrl+Home to extend the selection from the insertion point to the beginning of the document or Ctrl+End to extend it from the insertion point to the end of the document.

More stuff

If you ever find yourself selecting the wrong text, you can cancel the selection by pressing F8 or by clicking the insertion point anywhere in the document.

Show ¶

Displays symbols on the screen for each code you have entered in your document, including hard return, space, tab, indent, centering, flush right, soft hyphen, center page, and advance.

Pull-down menu

```
Show symbols for space, hard return, tab, etc. - Ctrl+Shift+F3
File  Edit  View  Insert  Format  Table  Graphics  Tools  Window  Help

                √Draft          Ctrl+F5
Times New Roman  Page           Alt+F5        eft    ▾ 1.0  ▾ Tables    ▾ Columns    ▾ 91% ▾
                 Two Page

                 Zoom...

                √Toolbar
                √Power Bar
                 Ruler Bar   Alt+Shift+F3
                √Status Bar
                 Hide Bars  Alt+Shift+F5

                √Graphics
                 Table Gridlines
                 Hidden Text
                 Show ¶    Ctrl+Shift+F3
                 Reveal Codes  Alt+F3

Insert      HP LaserJet 4M Plus/4M Plus (Win)   Select  November 20, 1994   2:56PM   Pg 1 Ln 1" Pos 1.5"
```

For keyboard kronies

 $\boxed{Ctrl}$ + $\boxed{Shift}$ + $\boxed{F3}$

More stuff

You can define which codes are to be represented by symbols on the screen by choosing Pr̲eferences from the E̲dit menu and then choosing D̲isplay. In the Display Preferences dialog box, choose the S̲how ¶ radio button. In the Symbols to Display area, deselect any of the check box options that you don't want displayed when Show ¶ from the V̲iew menu is activated.

Sort

Lets you rearrange text in alphabetic or numeric order. In Word-Perfect for Windows, you can sort lines of text (such as simple lists), paragraphs, records in a merge text data file, or rows in a table (see the sections "Merge" and "Tables" for more information).

Pull-down menu

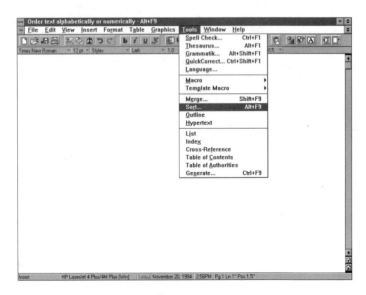

For keyboard kronies

Sorting information in WordPerfect for Windows

Sorting is based on keys, which indicate what specific information should be used to alphabetize or numerically reorder the text. You might have a list that contains your coworkers' names and telephone numbers, for example, and you want to sort the list alphabetically by last name. You tell WordPerfect for Windows to use the last name of each person as the sorting key. When you sort information with WordPerfect for Windows, you can define more than one sorting key. If your list of names and telephone numbers contains several Smiths and Joneses, you can define a second key that indicates how you want the duplicates to be arranged (by first name, for example).

To sort information in WordPerfect for Windows, follow these steps:

1. Open the document that contains the information you want to sort by choosing Open from the File menu.

2. If you want to sort a table or parallel columns, position the insertion point somewhere in the table or the columns. If you want to sort specific lines or paragraphs in a document, select just the lines or paragraphs (see the section "Select (Text)" for more information).

3. Choose Sort from the Tools menu (or press Alt+F9) to open the Sort dialog box.

4. If you want to save the sorted information in a file other than the current document file, use the Output File option to indicate which file to use.

5. Select the type of sort you want to use (such as First word in a line) in the Defined Sorts list box.

6. If you want uppercase letters sorted before lowercase letters, choose Uppercase First in the Options pop-up menu to put a checkmark in front of the option.

7. If you want to be able to restore your document to its original order by choosing Undo (Ctrl+Z) after sorting it, choose Allow Undo in the Options pop-up menu to put a checkmark in front of the option.

8. Choose Sort or press Enter to begin sorting.

Defining all sorts of new sorts

WordPerfect 6.1 ships the definitions for the most common types of sorts that you may use. In some situations, you may have to create your own sort definition, as follows:

1. Choose Sort from the Tools menu (or press Alt+F9) to open the Sort dialog box.

2. Choose the New button in the Sort dialog box to open the New Sort dialog box.

3. Replace <User Defined Sort> in the Sort Name text box with the name of the sort you're defining, which you want to appear in the Defined Sorts list box of the Sort dialog box.

4. If necessary, change the type of sort by choosing the appropriate radio button under Sort By. You can sort by Line, Paragraph, Merge Record, Table Row, or Column.

5. Define the first key by making any necessary changes to the Type, Sort Order, Field, Line, Word, and Cell (when you're performing a Table sort) settings for Key 1.

   By default, WordPerfect for Windows performs an Alpha sort in ascending order (from A to Z) based on the first word in the first line of the first field (or cell, when you're performing a Table sort).

6. To sort by another key, choose Add Key. Then change any of the settings that need modifying for Key 2.

7. Repeat step 6 until you have defined all the sort keys you want. (Extra keys are necessary only when the previous key has duplicates and you want to tell WordPerfect for Windows how to treat them — such as sorting by first name when you have duplicate last names.)

8. Choose OK or press Enter to close the New Sort dialog box and return to the Sort dialog box, where your new sort definition is displayed in the Defined Sorts list box.

9. To use the new definition in sorting, make sure it's selected in the Defined Sorts list box; then choose Sort. To return to your document without using the new sort definition, choose Close instead.

More stuff

The "key" to understanding sorting in WordPerfect for Windows
is to understand that the program divides information into fields
and records, based on different types of sorts, as shown in this
list:

- In a Line sort, each line terminated by a hard return is
  considered to be a record. These records can be subdivided into fields (separated by tabs) and words (separated
  by spaces, slashes, or hyphens).

- In a Paragraph sort, each paragraph that ends in two or
  more hard returns is a record. These records can be
  subdivided into lines (separated by soft returns), fields
  (separated by tabs), and words (separated by spaces,
  slashes, or hyphens).

- In a Merge Record sort, each record ends with an
  ENDRECORD merge code. These records can be subdivided
  into fields (separated by ENDFIELD codes), lines (separated by hard returns), and words (separated by spaces,
  slashes, or hyphens).

- In a (Parallel) Column sort, each record is one row of
  parallel columns. (See the "Columns" section for definitions
  of types of columns.) These records can be subdivided into
  columns (separated by a hard page), lines (separated by
  soft or hard returns), and words (separated by spaces,
  slashes, or hyphens).

- In a Table sort, each record is one row. These records can
  be subdivided into cells (numbered from left to right
  beginning with one), lines (separated by hard returns), and
  words (separated by spaces, slashes, or hyphens).

Spell Check

Lets you eliminate all those embarrassing spelling errors. The
WordPerfect for Windows Spell Checker also locates double
words (repeated words) and words with weird capitalization.

Pull-down menu

Check for misspelled words, double words, irregular capitalization - Ctrl+F1

| File | Edit | View | Insert | Format | Table | Graphics | **Tools** | Window | Help |

Times New Roman | 12 pt | Styles | Left | 1.0

Spell Check...   Ctrl+F1
Thesaurus...   Alt+F1
Grammatik...   Alt+Shift+F1
QuickCorrect... Ctrl+Shift+F1
Language...

Macro   ▶
Template Macro   ▶

Merge...   Shift+F9
Sort...   Alt+F9
Outline
Hypertext

List
Index
Cross-Reference
Table of Contents
Table of Authorities
Generate...   Ctrl+F9

Insert   HP LaserJet 4 Plus/4M Plus (Win)   Select November 20, 1994   2:56PM   Pg 1 Ln 1" Pos 1.5"

For keyboard kronies

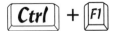

For mouse maniacs

Click ▦ on the WordPerfect 6.1 for Windows toolbar.

Spell checking a document

To check the spelling in your document, follow these steps:

1. To check the spelling of a word or page, position the insertion point somewhere in that word or on that page. To check the spelling from a particular word in the text to the end of the document, position the insertion point on that word. To check the spelling of the entire document, you can position the insertion point anywhere in the document.

2. Choose Spell Check from the Tools menu (or press Ctrl+F1) to open the Spell Check window.

3. By default, the program spell checks the entire document (unless text is selected, in which case the program opts to check only the selection). To change the amount of text that is spell checked, choose the appropriate command from the Chec<u>k</u> pull-down menu in the Spell Check menu bar. The commands for specific text are <u>W</u>ord; Senten<u>c</u>e; <u>P</u>aragraph; P<u>a</u>ge; <u>D</u>ocument; To <u>E</u>nd of Document; <u>S</u>elected Text; <u>T</u>ext Entry Box; or <u>N</u>umber of Pages.

4. Choose <u>S</u>tart or press Enter to begin spell checking.

When the Spell Check locates a word it cannot find in its dictionary, the Spell Check highlights the word in the text and displays the word at the top of the Spell Check window after the Not found message. The Spell Check then lists all suggestions for replacing the unknown (and potentially misspelled) word in the Sugg<u>e</u>stions list box. The first suggestion in this list is also shown in the Replace <u>W</u>ith text box.

5. To replace the unknown word with the word located in the Replace With text box, choose <u>R</u>eplace or press Enter. To replace the unknown word with another proposed word from the Sugg<u>e</u>stions list box, select the proposed word. After it appears in the Replace <u>W</u>ith text box, choose <u>R</u>eplace or press Enter.

To skip the unknown word one time only and continue spell checking, choose Skip <u>O</u>nce.

To skip this unknown word and every other occurrence of it throughout the document, choose Skip <u>A</u>lways.

To add the unknown word to the supplementary spelling dictionary (so that the Spell Check skips the word in this and every other document), choose A<u>d</u>d.

To edit the unknown word while in the text, click the word in the document to activate the document window. Then make your changes. When you're ready to resume spell checking, choose <u>R</u>esume in the Spell Check window.

There may be no suggestions for the unknown word offered in the Replace <u>W</u>ith text box and Sugg<u>e</u>stions list box. Or maybe none of the suggestions is anywhere close to the word you tried to spell. If this occurs, enter a best-guess spelling in the Replace <u>W</u>ith text box and then choose S<u>u</u>ggest to have the Spell Check look up the word.

6. When the Spell Check locates the occurrence of a duplicate word in the text, it highlights both words and suggests just one of the words as the replacement in the Replace With text box. To disable duplicate word checking, choose Duplicate Words from the Options pull-down menu on the Spell Check menu bar.

7. When the Spell Check locates a word that uses irregular capitalization, it highlights this word and makes various alternative capitalization suggestions in the Replace With text box and Suggestions list box. To disable irregular capitalization checking, choose Irregular Capitalization from the Options pull-down menu on the Spell Check menu bar.

8. When the Spell Check encounters a word with numbers in it (such as B52 or RX7), the Spell Check highlights the unknown word and displays whatever suggestions it can come up with in the Replace With text box and Suggestions list box. To disable spell checking of words with numbers, choose Words with Numbers from the Options pull-down menu on the Spell Check menu bar.

9. When the Spell Check finishes checking the document (or the part you indicated), it displays a Spell Check dialog box informing you that the spell check has been completed and asks whether you want to close the Spell Check. Choose Yes or press Enter to close the Spell Check window and return to the document. You can also close the Spell Check at any time by choosing Close or double-clicking its Control-menu button.

More stuff

Save your document immediately after spell checking it to ensure that you don't lose the edits made by way of the Spell Check. For more information about this command, see Chapter 7 of *WordPerfect For Windows For Dummies.*

Status Bar

Keeps you informed of lots of useful information like whether you're in Insert or Typeover mode, which printer is selected, the current date and time, and the current page, line, and cursor position.

Pull-down menu

For mouse maniacs

To hide the Status bar, click the Status bar with the secondary mouse button and then choose Hide Status Bar from the QuickMenu.

More stuff

You can change what information is displayed on the Status bar and how it is displayed by choosing Preferences on the Status bar QuickMenu. To add or remove items, select or deselect their check boxes in the Status Bar Items list box. To rearrange the order of the items on the Status bar, drag their buttons to new positions. To resize an item, position the mouse pointer on the item's border and, when the pointer changes to a double-headed arrow, drag the border in the appropriate direction. To change the font and font size used on the Status bar, choose the Options button and then select the desired font face and font size in the Font and Size list boxes, respectively.

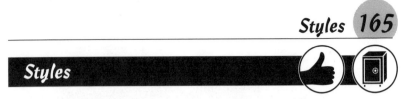

Styles

Lets you format various parts of a document in the same manner by simply applying the appropriate style to the text. By using styles, you don't have to use individual formatting commands every time you format text.

Pull-down menu

For keyboard kronies

[Alt] + [F8]

Styles à la QuickStyle

You can create a style for your document by choosing each format setting from the WordPerfect for Windows pull-down menu in the Style Editor. The easiest way to create the style, however, is by example using the QuickCreate feature, as shown in these steps:

1. Format the document text exactly as you want it to appear in the style, including fonts, sizes, attributes, alignment, justification, and so on.

2. Select the formatted text. Be sure to include as part of your selection all the secret codes that change the font or font size or otherwise format this selected text!

3. Choose Styles from the Format menu (or press Alt+F8) to open the Style List dialog box.

4. Choose QuickStyle to open the QuickStyle dialog box.

5. Enter a name for your new style (such as 1st Head) in the Style Name text box. The name can be as long as 12 characters. Then press Tab.

6. Enter a description of the new style (such as 50-point bold Helvetica) in the Description text box.

7. By default, WordPerfect for Windows creates a Paragraph style. This means that the program applies the formatting to the entire paragraph. To create a Character style instead (the program applies the formatting to only the selected text), choose the Character radio button.

8. Choose OK or press Enter to close the QuickStyle dialog box and return to the Style List dialog box. Your new style is now listed and selected.

9. To apply your brand-new style to the text that is currently selected in the document, choose Apply. To close the Style List dialog box without assigning the style to the selected text, choose Close.

More stuff

To turn on a style before you type the text, position the insertion point in the text where you want the style formatting to begin. Then open the Style List dialog box by choosing Styles from the Format menu or by pressing Alt+F8. Select the style in the Name list box and choose Apply or press Enter. Now you can type the text. To turn off the style in a new paragraph, open the Style List dialog box and select <None> in the Name list box. Then choose Apply or press Enter.

To apply a paragraph style to an existing paragraph of text, position the insertion point somewhere in that paragraph. Then select the style in the Name list box found in the Style List dialog box and choose Apply or press Enter.

 For more information about this command, see Chapter 12 of *WordPerfect For Windows For Dummies.*

Suppress

Lets you temporarily stop the printing of a header, footer, or page number on a single page of the document.

Pull-down menu

Turn off headers, footers, etc., for the current page

File   Edit   View   Insert   Format   Table   Graphics   Tools   Window   Help

Times New Roman   12 pt   StyA   Tables   Columns   91%

Font...   F9
Line
Paragraph

Page   ▶   Center...
Document   Suppress...
Columns   Delay Codes...
                   Force Page...
Make It Fit Expert...   Keep Text Together...
Drop Cap Ctrl+Shift+C
                   Border/Fill...
Header/Footer...   Numbering...
Watermark...
                   Subdivide Page...
Margins...   Ctrl+F8   Binding/Duplex...
Justification   Paper Size...
Typesetting

Envelope...
Labels...

QuickFormat...
Styles...   Alt+F8

Insert   HP LaserJet 4 Plus/4M Plus (Win)   Select   November 20, 1994   2:59PM   Pg 1 Ln 1" Pos 1.5"

This header is suppressed!

Suppress lets you stop page numbering, headers, footers, or watermarks from printing on a particular page. To do so, just open the Suppress dialog box and choose the check boxes for all the page elements that should not appear on the current page.

When you're suppressing normal page numbering on the current page, you can choose the Print Page Number at Bottom Center on Current Page option by putting an X in its check box. This option prints the page number in the center near the bottom of just that single page.

More stuff

Before choosing this command, position the insertion point somewhere on the page where you want the page elements to be temporarily suspended.

For more information about this command, see Chapter 10 of *WordPerfect For Windows For Dummies.*

Tab Set

Lets you change the tabs in your document.

Pull-down menu

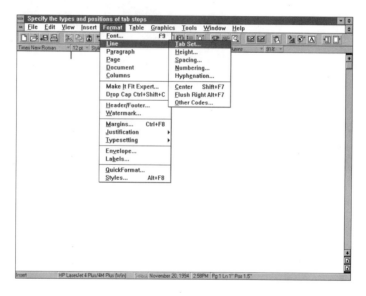

QuickMenus

You can change the tabs by using the Tab Set dialog box. To do so, click the ruler bar (displayed by choosing Ruler Bar from the View menu) with the secondary mouse button (the right mouse button for right-handers, and the left mouse button for lefties).

For mouse maniacs

You can change tabs directly on the ruler bar (see the "Ruler Bar" section for details). You can also display the Tab Set dialog box and change the tabs by double-clicking any of the tab icons displayed on the ruler bar.

The changing of the tabs

You can change tabs anywhere in the document text. To set uniform tabs for the document, follow these steps:

1. Position the insertion point somewhere in the first paragraph where the new tab settings will take effect.

2. Choose Line from the Format menu and then choose Tab Set from the cascading menu to open the Tab Set dialog box.

3. Choose Clear All to delete all the current tabs.

4. Select the type of tabs you want to set in the Type pop-up list (Left, Center, Right, Decimal, Dot Left, Dot Center, Dot Right, or Dot Decimal).

5. Choose Position and enter the distance between the first tab and the left margin or the left edge of the page. You can also select this distance with the up- and down-arrow buttons. Zero inches puts the first tab in line with the left margin.

6. Choose Repeat Every by putting an X in its check box and, using its text box, enter a measurement for how far apart each tab stop should be. You can also select this measurement with the up- and down-arrow buttons.

7. If you want the tabs to always remain fixed, even if you change the left margin, select the Left Edge of Paper (Absolute) radio button. Otherwise, the Left Margin (Relative) radio button is chosen by default.

8. To change the dot leader character when you're using a dot leader tab (such as Dot Left, Dot Center, Dot Right, or Dot Decimal), choose Dot Leader Character. Then enter the new character in the text box. To insert a character not available from the keyboard, press Ctrl+W and choose the WordPerfect Character (see the "WordPerfect Characters" section).

   To change the spacing between each dot, choose Space Between Characters and then enter the new distance in the text box. (Or you can select this measurement with the up- and down-arrow buttons.)

9. To change the alignment character when you're setting Decimal or Dot Decimal tabs, choose Character under Align Character and enter the new alignment characters in the text box.

10. Choose Set to move the insertion point to the end of the first tab measurement. Put an X in the Repeat Every check box, enter the distance that should separate each subsequent tab in its text box, and press Enter. As soon as you choose Set, WordPerfect for Windows uses the separation interval in the Repeat Every text box to indicate the location of the tabs across the ruler with the appropriate letters. You can also see the new tab settings take effect in your document text by looking at the text that shows behind the Tab Set dialog box.

11. Choose OK or press Enter to close the Tab Set dialog box and return to your document. You can now see your new uniform tab settings.

More stuff

You can also set individual tab settings in the Tab Set dialog box. Simply choose the type of tab and enter its position (relative to the left margin or the left edge of the paper) in the Position text box. Then choose Set to insert the tab on the tab ruler.

Keep in mind that instead of going through the rigmarole of changing tabs in the Tab Set dialog box, you can change the tabs on the ruler bar (see the "Ruler Bar" section for more information).

 For more information about this command, see Chapter 9 of
WordPerfect For Windows For Dummies.

Tables

Lets you set text in a tabular format by using a layout of columns
and rows, much like a spreadsheet. Tables not only superficially
resemble spreadsheets, in fact, but they can also accommodate
worksheets created with that type of software and can perform
most of the same functions. Moreover, the boxes formed by the
intersection of a column and a row are called *cells,* just as they
are in a spreadsheet. Each cell has a cell address that corre-
sponds to the letter of its column (from A to Z and then doubled,
as in AA, AB, and so on) and the number of its row (the first row
is 1). Therefore, the first cell in the upper left corner is A1 (because it's in column A and row 1).

Pull-down menu

For keyboard kronies

For mouse maniacs

Click the Tables button on the Power bar (see "Power Bar" for details) and drag through the tiny table grid until you have highlighted all the cells you want in the table. Then release the mouse button.

To change the width of a column in a table, position the mouse pointer somewhere on the border of the column you want to change. When the pointer changes to a double-headed arrow pointing to the left and right, drag the column border until the column is the width you want.

When you create a new table (or position the insertion point in any of the cells in an existing table), WordPerfect for Windows automatically switches to the Tables toolbar, which contains lots of useful buttons (such as Table Expert, Table Format, Lines/Fill, Number Type, and so on) for formatting the new table.

QuickMenus

The Table QuickMenu enables you to do lots of table-related stuff, such as format existing cells or insert or delete cells. You can also use the QuickMenu to display the formula bar when you create and calculate formulas in the cells.

Creating a table

To create a table, first indicate the number of columns and rows the table should have by following these steps:

1. Move the insertion point to the beginning of the new line in the document where you want the table to appear.

2. Choose Create from the Table menu or press F12 to open the Create Table dialog box.

3. By default, WordPerfect for Windows creates a table with three columns and one row. To accept this default table size, choose OK or press Enter. To create a table that has more columns and rows, enter the number of columns in the Columns text box and the number of rows in the Rows text box. Then choose OK or press Enter.

Entering text in a table

After creating the table structure, you can enter text in the various cells of the table. To enter text, position the insertion point in the cell (it's in the first cell by default) and begin typing. To advance to the next cell on the right, press Tab. To return to the previous cell, press Shift+Tab (which is a backward tab). When you reach the last cell in a row, pressing Tab moves you to the cell at the beginning of the next row. If you press Tab when the insertion point is in the last cell of a table, WordPerfect for Windows adds a blank row of cells to the table and positions the insertion point in the first cell in this new row.

More stuff

You can convert a table created with tabs or parallel columns into a WordPerfect for Windows table (see the "Columns" section for more information about parallel columns). To do so, select the lines of the tabular table or parallel columns and choose Create from the Table menu, which opens the Convert Table dialog box. Then choose either the Tabular Column or Parallel Column radio button under Create Table From and choose OK or press Enter.

For more information about this command, see Chapter 16 of *WordPerfect For Windows For Dummies.*

Thesaurus

Lets you find synonyms (words with similar meanings) and antonyms (words with opposite meanings) for many of the words you overuse in a document.

Pull-down menu

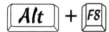

For keyboard kronies

[Alt] + [F8]

More stuff

To look up a word in the Thesaurus, position the insertion point somewhere in the word and then open the Thesaurus dialog box (press Alt+F1).

Keep in mind that when you replace a word with a synonym or antonym from the Thesaurus, WordPerfect for Windows makes no attempt to match the original tense or number in the text. So if you look up the word *jumped* in a document and select *leap* in the Thesaurus dialog box as its replacement, WordPerfect for Windows inserts *leap* without an *ed* (which you must then add yourself).

For more information about this command, see Chapter 7 of *WordPerfect For Windows For Dummies.*

Toolbars

Let you select WordPerfect 6.1 for Windows commands, insert stock text, launch new programs, or play macros by simply displaying the correct toolbar and then clicking the correct button. (In previous versions of WordPerfect for Windows, toolbars were known as Button bars.)

Pull-down menu

To display or hide the selected toolbar, choose the following View menu command:

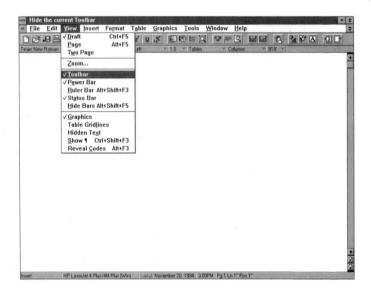

For mouse maniacs

To display a new toolbar, click the currently displayed toolbar with the secondary mouse button. Then drag to or click the name of the new toolbar in the toolbar QuickMenu that you want displayed.

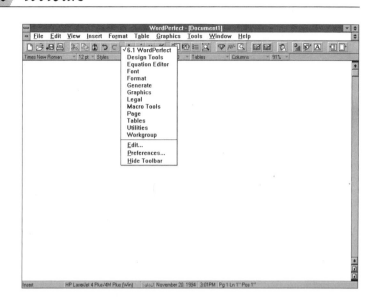

Moving the toolbar

You can move the toolbar by positioning the mouse pointer anywhere on the toolbar where there are no buttons — on the borders or in the extra gray space. As soon as the mouse pointer
changes into a cupped hand, you can drag the toolbar to a new
position.

If you release the mouse button when the outline of the toolbar is
somewhere in the document window, the toolbar appears as a
palette in its own window; you can resize this palette window and
move it around the document window as you would resize and
move any other window. To hide the toolbar, double-click the
Control-menu button in the toolbar window. You can redisplay
the toolbar by choosing Toolbar from the View menu.

You can also *dock* the toolbar along any one of the four borders
of the program window. To do so, drag the outline (border) of the
toolbar to one edge of the program window until the outline of
the toolbar changes shape and conforms to the window's edge.
Then release the mouse button.

Changing how the buttons appear

Normally, a toolbar displays only icons without displaying any text. To change the appearance of the buttons, follow these steps:

1. If the toolbar isn't already displayed on the screen, choose Toolbar from the View pull-down menu.

2. Click the toolbar with the secondary mouse button (the right button if you're a right-handed mouser or the left button if you're a left-handed mouser) and choose Preferences from the toolbar QuickMenu.

3. Choose Options in the Toolbar Preferences dialog box.

4. To display text on the buttons instead of a picture, choose the Text radio button under Appearance. To display both text and a picture on the buttons, choose the Picture and Text radio button.

5. To change the font of the text that appears on the buttons, choose a new font in the Font Face list box.

6. To change the size of the text on the buttons, choose a new size in the Font Size list box or enter a new size in the text box.

7. To change the location of the toolbar (without having to drag it around with the mouse), choose the Left, Top, Right, Bottom, or Palette radio button.

   When you choose any option other than Palette, the Maximum Number of Rows/Columns To Show option is available. With this option, you can enter in the text box the maximum number of rows (if the toolbar is at the top or bottom of the screen) or columns (if the bar is on the left or right) that you want WordPerfect for Windows to display.

8. By default, WordPerfect for Windows displays on the WordPerfect title bar the name of each button and a description of its function when you position the mouse pointer over it. If you don't want this display, deselect the Show QuickTips check box.

9. To add scroll buttons that enable you to scroll through the buttons of a toolbar containing too many buttons to be displayed in one screen, select the Show Scroll Bar option to put an X in its check box.

10. Choose OK or press Enter to close the Toolbar Options dialog box and then choose Close in the Toolbar Preferences dialog box.

To save room on your screen and still be able to distinguish the buttons easily, make sure that the Show QuickTips check box is selected; then just position the mouse pointer over a button to find out what it does.

Creating a custom toolbar

WordPerfect for Windows makes it easy to create your own toolbars. Follow these steps:

1. If the toolbar isn't already displayed on the screen, choose Toolbar from the View pull-down menu.

2. Click the toolbar with the secondary mouse button and then choose Preferences from the toolbar QuickMenu.

3. Choose Create in the Toolbar Preferences dialog box.

4. By default, WordPerfect for Windows stores the new toolbar with the current template. If you want to store the toolbar with whatever template is the default (Standard is the default unless you have changed it), first choose Template. Then choose the Default Template radio button in the Toolbar Location dialog box and choose OK or press Enter.

5. Type the name for your new toolbar in the New Toolbar Name text box. Then choose OK to open the Toolbar Editor, which shows the name of your new toolbar.

6. To add a button, choose the appropriate radio button under Add a Button To. (Activate a Feature adds a menu command, Play a Keyboard Script inserts text, Launch a Program starts a new program from WordPerfect for Windows, and Play a Macro executes a macro.)

   If you choose the Activate a Feature radio button, select the name of the pull-down menu (which includes the command that you want to add) in the Feature Categories list box. Then choose the particular command or feature in the Features list box and choose Add Button or press Enter.

   When you select a command in the Features list box, the program displays the icon and text used for that button with an explanation of what the button does. (This display is located under Add Button.) Then, instead of choosing Add Button or pressing Enter to insert the new button on the toolbar, you can click the feature in the list box and drag the hand-holding-a-button mouse pointer to the place on the toolbar where you want the new button to be added.

If you choose the Play a Keyboard Script radio button, choose the Type The Script This Button Plays option. Type the text that you want to insert in the document when you click the button and then choose Add Script or press Enter.

If you chose either the Launch a Program or the Play a Macro radio button, choose Select File, Add Macro, or Add Template Macro. In the Select File dialog box, choose the program file or macro file that you want the button to execute. Then press Enter to place the new button in the toolbar.

7. Repeat Step 6 until you have added all the buttons that you want to appear on the new toolbar.

8. To change the position of a button that you have added to the toolbar, press and drag the button to the place on the toolbar where you want it to appear and then release the mouse button.

9. To group two or more buttons together, you insert a space between a pair of buttons. To do so, click the Separator icon in the Toolbar Editor dialog box. When the mouse pointer changes into the hand-holding-a-separator, drag this pointer to the toolbar until it's between the buttons that you want to separate with a space and then release.

10. When you have finished adding and arranging buttons on the new toolbar, choose OK to close the Toolbar Editor dialog box and return to the Toolbar Preferences dialog box. Your new toolbar appears in the Available Toolbars list box.

11. To select the new toolbar, choose Select in the Toolbar Preferences dialog box. To leave current whatever toolbar was selected at the time you created your new toolbar, choose Close instead.

More stuff

Unlike feature bars (see the "Feature Bars" section), which have keyboard shortcuts so that you don't have to use a mouse to select buttons, buttons on a toolbar are accessible only by clicking the primary mouse button.

For more information about this command, see Chapter 2 of *WordPerfect For Windows For Dummies*.

Two Page View

Lets you see two pages of a document on the screen at one time.

Pull-down menu

Display two pages at a time

| File | Edit | View | Insert | Format | Table | Graphics | Tools | Window | Help |

√ Draft   Ctrl+F5
Page   Alt+F5
Two Page

Zoom...

√ Toolbar
√ Power Bar
Ruler Bar   Alt+Shift+F3
√ Status Bar
Hide Bars Alt+Shift+F5

√ Graphics
Table Gridlines
Hidden Text
Show ¶   Ctrl+Shift+F3
Reveal Codes   Alt+F3

Insert   HP LaserJet 4 Plus/4M Plus (Win)   Select   November 20, 1994   3:03PM   Pg 1 Ln 1" Pos 1"

More stuff

When you use two-page view in WordPerfect for Windows, you can edit the text and graphics as you would edit them on a nor-mal-size page (if you can see the stuff that needs editing). You cannot, however, use the Zoom command to zoom in on a part of the two-page spread. To use the Zoom command, you must switch back to page view or draft view (see the sections "Draft View," "Page View," and "Zoom").

Typeover

Typeover is the typing mode opposite the default typing mode, which is Insert. In Typeover mode, the new characters you type on a line eat up the existing characters rather than push the existing characters to the right of the newly typed text (as is the case when you're using Insert mode).

More stuff

You can switch between Insert and Typeover modes by pressing Insert. WordPerfect for Windows always tells you when you have switched into Typeover mode by replacing Insert with Typeover on the Status bar.

For more information about this command, see Chapter 4 of *WordPerfect For Windows For Dummies.*

Undelete

Restores at the insertion point's current position any of the last three text deletions you made in your document.

Pull-down menu

![Screenshot of WordPerfect for Windows with the Edit menu open. The title bar reads "Restore one of your last three deletions - Ctrl+Shift+Z". The Edit menu shows: Undo Ctrl+Z, Redo Ctrl+Shift+R, Undo/Redo History..., Undelete... Ctrl+Shift+Z, Repeat..., Cut Ctrl+X, Copy Ctrl+C, Paste Ctrl+V, Append, Select, Paste Special..., Links..., Object..., Find and Replace... F2, Go To... Ctrl+G, Convert Case, Preferences... The status bar at bottom shows: Insert | HP LaserJet 4 Plus/4M Plus (Win) | Select | November 20, 1994 | 3:04PM | Pg 1 Ln 1" Pos 1"]

For keyboard kronies

$\boxed{Ctrl} + \boxed{Shift} + \boxed{Z}$

More stuff

When you press Ctrl+Shift+Z (or choose Undelete from the Edit menu), WordPerfect for Windows displays the Undelete dialog box. This box displays the last deletion you made as highlighted text at the insertion point's current position. To restore this text to the document, choose Restore. To see a previous deletion (up to the third one you made), choose Previous. To return to a deletion you have already seen, choose Next. When the text you want to restore appears, choose Restore. If the text never appears, choose Cancel or press Esc to close the Undelete dialog box.

For more information about this command, see Chapter 4 of *WordPerfect For Windows For Dummies.*

Underline

Underlines selected text in the document.

For keyboard kronies

$\boxed{Ctrl} + \boxed{U}$

For mouse maniacs

Click $\boxed{u}$ on the WordPerfect 6.1 for Windows toolbar.

More stuff

You can underline text before or after you type it, just as you can with bold and italics (see the "Bold" section to get the general idea). To get rid of underlining in the text, open the Reveal Codes window and delete either the [Und> or the <Und] secret code that encloses the text.

For more information about this command, see Chapter 8 of *WordPerfect For Windows For Dummies.*

Undo

Restores the document to its previous state before you messed it up.

Pull-down menu

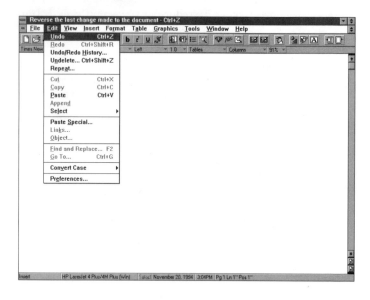

For keyboard kronies

To undo your last action press

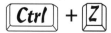

To redo your last action press

For mouse maniacs

To undo your last action, click on the WordPerfect 6.1 for Windows toolbar. To redo your last action, click ⟳ instead.

More stuff

In WordPerfect 6.1 for Windows, you can undo (and redo) up to 300 of your past actions (wow!) — although WordPerfect for Windows is really only set up to undo the last ten actions when you start using the program. To increase the number of Undos and Redos allowed, choose Undo/Redo History on the Edit menu to open the Undo/Redo History dialog box. Then choose the Options button and enter the new number of Undos/Redos in the Number of Undo/Redo Items text box in the Undo/Redo Options dialog box.

To undo more than one action at a time, open the Undo/Redo History dialog box and then select the last item in the Undo list box that you want undone (WordPerfect for Windows will automatically select all items above the one you select) and click the Undo button. To redo more than one item, you perform the same sequence in the Redo list box and then choose the Redo button.

For more information about this command, see Chapter 2 of *WordPerfect For Windows For Dummies*.

Watermark

Inserts background text or graphics in a document that other text can be printed over and can still be read.

Pull-down menu

Creating a watermark

Creating a watermark is similar to creating a header or footer.
(That's why they put Watermark right under Header/Footer on
the Format menu.) To create a watermark, follow these steps:

1. Place the insertion point on the first page on which you
   want to have a watermark.

2. Choose Watermark from the Format menu to open the Watermark dialog box.

3. Choose Create to create Watermark A. (To create a second
   watermark, select Watermark B before you choose Create.)

   WordPerfect for Windows then opens a special Watermark
   window and displays the Watermark feature bar.

4. To add a graphics image to the watermark, choose Image
   on the Watermark feature bar and then choose a graphics
   file in the Insert Image dialog box. WordPerfect for Windows inserts the image as light gray in the document and
   displays the graphics box feature bar. Edit the light gray
   graphics image as you see fit and then choose Close, which
   closes the graphics box feature bar and returns to the Watermark feature bar.

5. To add text to your watermark, type the text in the Watermark window or open the document that contains the text. To do so, choose File on the Watermark features bar and then select the filename in the Insert File dialog box.

6. By default, if you add a watermark to your document, WordPerfect for Windows adds it to all pages in the document. To add the watermark to only the even or odd pages, choose Pages on the Watermark feature bar. Then choose the Odd Pages radio button or the Even Pages radio button.

7. When you finish entering and formatting the watermark text or adding the watermark graphics images, choose Close on the Watermark feature bar. The Watermark window and Watermark feature bar both close and you return to your document.

More stuff

Any watermark you add to a document is visible on the screen only when the program is in page view or two-page view. When you switch to draft view, the watermark image and text disappear from the screen.

You can suppress the printing of a watermark on a specific page just as you can suppress a header or footer from printing (see the "Suppress" section for details).

Widow/Orphan (See "Keep Text Together")

Window

The Window commands let you switch between documents that are open in different windows and let you arrange all the open document windows on one screen. The arrangement of the windows can be overlapping or side-by-side. The Window pull-down menu also shows all the files that are currently open but that may not be active.

Pull-down menu

(WordPerfect screen showing the Window pull-down menu open with Cascade, Tile Horizontal, Tile Vertical, and √1 Document1 options)

More stuff

To make another document window active, open the <u>W</u>indow menu and then type the underlined number given to the document window or click the number or filename with the mouse.

Choose <u>T</u>ile Horizontal, Tile <u>V</u>ertical, or <u>C</u>ascade from the <u>Win</u>dow menu to arrange all the open windows. (You can have as many as nine windows open if your computer has enough memory.) <u>T</u>ile Horizontal places the windows side by side; Tile <u>V</u>ertical places the windows one on top of the other; <u>C</u>ascade places them one in front of the other with the title bars of each one showing.

For more information about this command, see Chapter 14 of *WordPerfect For Windows For Dummies.*

WordPerfect 6.0a Menu

Lets you switch the menu bar between the new 6.1 and old 6.0a menu arrangement.

For mouse maniacs

To change to WordPerfect for Windows 6.0a menus, click the menu bar with the secondary mouse button and choose <WPWin 6.0a Menu> on the menu bar QuickMenu. To change back to the new WordPerfect for Windows 6.1 menus, click the menu bar with the secondary mouse button and choose <WPWin 6.1 Menu> option on the menu bar QuickMenu.

WordPerfect Characters

Lets you insert special characters that are not available from the regular keyboard (such as weird foreign language and math and science symbols).

Pull-down menu

For keyboard kronies

$\boxed{\textbf{Ctrl}} + \boxed{\textbf{W}}$

More stuff

To insert a WordPerfect character into the text of your document or into a text box in a dialog box, position the insertion point where you want the character to appear. Then open the WordPerfect Characters dialog box (you must press Ctrl+W when you're in a dialog box). Choose the character set you want to use in the Character Set pop-up list and then select the character to use in the Characters list box. To insert the selected character and leave the WordPerfect Characters dialog box open, choose Insert (or double-click the character). To insert the selected character and also close the dialog box, choose Insert and Close.

Each WordPerfect character is assigned a set number plus a character number. This number is shown in the Number text box when you select a character in the Characters list box. If you already know the set number and character number for the character you want to use, select it by simply entering the two numbers in the Number text box and separate them with a comma.

Zoom

Lets you change the size of the screen display as you're running WordPerfect for Windows in draft view or page view.

Pull-down menu

Zoom document in or out

| File | Edit | View | Insert | Format | Table | Graphics | Tools | Window | Help |

Draft   Ctrl+F5
√ Page   Alt+F5
  Two Page

  Zoom...

√ Toolbar
√ Power Bar
  Ruler Bar Alt+Shift+F3
√ Status Bar
  Hide Bars Alt+Shift+F5

√ Graphics
  Table Gridlines
  Hidden Text
  Show ¶   Ctrl+Shift+F3
  Reveal Codes   Alt+F3

Times New Roman   Left   1.0   Tables   Columns   100%

Insert   Apple LaserWriter II NTX (Win)   Select   September 11, 1994   7:55PM   Pg 1 Ln 1" Pos 2.5"

For mouse maniacs

Click the Zoom button on the Power bar and drag to the Zoom command you want to use. Click 🔍 on the WordPerfect 6.1 for Windows toolbar to toggle between full page and the current zoom setting.

More stuff

Select the Margin Width radio button to have WordPerfect for Windows fill the document window with text from margin to margin and with minimal white space. Use Page Width to display the entire width of the document within the document window. Use Full Page to display the entire length of the document within the document window.

For more information about this command, see Chapter 20 of *WordPerfect For Windows For Dummies*.

Index

(continued)

(continued)

• Z •

Notes

Notes

Notes

Here's a complete listing of IDG Books' ...For Dummies® titles

Title	Author	ISBN	Price
DATABASE			
Access 2 For Dummies®	by Scott Palmer	ISBN: 1-56884-090-X	$19.95 USA/$26.95 Canada
Access Programming For Dummies®	by Rob Krumm	ISBN: 1-56884-091-8	$19.95 USA/$26.95 Canada
Approach 3 For Windows® For Dummies®	by Doug Lowe	ISBN: 1-56884-233-3	$19.99 USA/$26.95 Canada
dBASE For DOS For Dummies®	by Scott Palmer & Michael Stabler	ISBN: 1-56884-188-4	$19.95 USA/$26.95 Canada
dBASE For Windows® For Dummies®	by Scott Palmer	ISBN: 1-56884-179-5	$19.95 USA/$26.95 Canada
dBASE 5 For Windows® Programming For Dummies®	by Ted Coombs & Jason Coombs	ISBN: 1-56884-215-5	$19.99 USA/$26.99 Canada
FoxPro 2.6 For Windows® For Dummies®	by John Kaufeld	ISBN: 1-56884-187-6	$19.95 USA/$26.95 Canada
Paradox 5 For Windows® For Dummies®	by John Kaufeld	ISBN: 1-56884-185-X	$19.95 USA/$26.95 Canada
DESKTOP PUBLISHING/ILLUSTRATION/GRAPHICS			
CorelDRAW! 5 For Dummies®	by Deke McClelland	ISBN: 1-56884-157-4	$19.95 USA/$26.95 Canada
CorelDRAW! For Dummies®	by Deke McClelland	ISBN: 1-56884-042-X	$19.95 USA/$26.95 Canada
Desktop Publishing & Design For Dummies®	by Roger C. Parker	ISBN: 1-56884-234-1	$19.99 USA/$26.99 Canada
Harvard Graphics 2 For Windows® For Dummies®	by Roger C. Parker	ISBN: 1-56884-092-6	$19.95 USA/$26.95 Canada
PageMaker 5 For Macs® For Dummies®	by Galen Gruman & Deke McClelland	ISBN: 1-56884-178-7	$19.95 USA/$26.95 Canada
PageMaker 5 For Windows® For Dummies®	by Deke McClelland & Galen Gruman	ISBN: 1-56884-160-4	$19.95 USA/$26.95 Canada
Photoshop 3 For Macs® For Dummies®	by Deke McClelland	ISBN: 1-56884-208-2	$19.99 USA/$26.99 Canada
QuarkXPress 3.3 For Dummies®	by Galen Gruman & Barbara Assadi	ISBN: 1-56884-217-1	$19.99 USA/$26.99 Canada
FINANCE/PERSONAL FINANCE/TEST TAKING REFERENCE			
Everyday Math For Dummies™	by Charles Seiter	ISBN: 1-56884-248-2	$14.99 USA/$22.99 Canada
Personal Finance For Dummies® For Canadians	by Eric Tyson & Tony Martin	ISBN: 1-56884-378-X	$18.99 USA/$24.99 Canada
QuickBooks 3 For Dummies®	by Stephen L. Nelson	ISBN: 1-56884-227-9	$19.99 USA/$26.99 Canada
Quicken 8 For DOS For Dummies,® 2nd Edition	by Stephen L. Nelson	ISBN: 1-56884-210-4	$19.95 USA/$26.95 Canada
Quicken 5 For Macs® For Dummies®	by Stephen L. Nelson	ISBN: 1-56884-211-2	$19.95 USA/$26.95 Canada
Quicken 4 For Windows® For Dummies,® 2nd Edition	by Stephen L. Nelson	ISBN: 1-56884-209-0	$19.95 USA/$26.95 Canada
Taxes For Dummies,™ 1995 Edition	by Eric Tyson & David J. Silverman	ISBN: 1-56884-220-1	$14.99 USA/$20.99 Canada
The GMAT® For Dummies™	by Suzee Vlk, Series Editor	ISBN: 1-56884-376-3	$14.99 USA/$20.99 Canada
The GRE® For Dummies™	by Suzee Vlk, Series Editor	ISBN: 1-56884-375-5	$14.99 USA/$20.99 Canada
Time Management For Dummies™	by Jeffrey J. Mayer	ISBN: 1-56884-360-7	$16.99 USA/$22.99 Canada
TurboTax For Windows® For Dummies®	by Gail A. Helsel, CPA	ISBN: 1-56884-228-7	$19.99 USA/$26.99 Canada
GROUPWARE/INTEGRATED			
ClarisWorks For Macs® For Dummies®	by Frank Higgins	ISBN: 1-56884-363-1	$19.99 USA/$26.99 Canada
Lotus Notes For Dummies®	by Pat Freeland & Stephen Londergan	ISBN: 1-56884-212-0	$19.95 USA/$26.95 Canada
Microsoft® Office 4 For Windows® For Dummies®	by Roger C. Parker	ISBN: 1-56884-183-3	$19.95 USA/$26.95 Canada
Microsoft® Works 3 For Windows® For Dummies®	by David C. Kay	ISBN: 1-56884-214-7	$19.99 USA/$26.99 Canada
SmartSuite 3 For Dummies®	by Jan Weingarten & John Weingarten	ISBN: 1-56884-367-4	$19.99 USA/$26.99 Canada
INTERNET/COMMUNICATIONS/NETWORKING			
America Online® For Dummies,® 2nd Edition	by John Kaufeld	ISBN: 1-56884-933-8	$19.99 USA/$26.99 Canada
CompuServe For Dummies,® 2nd Edition	by Wallace Wang	ISBN: 1-56884-937-0	$19.99 USA/$26.99 Canada
Modems For Dummies,® 2nd Edition	by Tina Rathbone	ISBN: 1-56884-223-6	$19.99 USA/$26.99 Canada
MORE Internet For Dummies®	by John R. Levine & Margaret Levine Young	ISBN: 1-56884-164-7	$19.99 USA/$26.95 Canada
MORE Modems & On-line Services For Dummies®	by Tina Rathbone	ISBN: 1-56884-365-8	$19.99 USA/$26.99 Canada
Mosaic For Dummies,® Windows Edition	by David Angell & Brent Heslop	ISBN: 1-56884-242-2	$19.99 USA/$26.99 Canada
NetWare For Dummies,® 2nd Edition	by Ed Tittel, Deni Connor & Earl Follis	ISBN: 1-56884-369-0	$19.99 USA/$26.99 Canada
Networking For Dummies®	by Doug Lowe	ISBN: 1-56884-079-9	$19.95 USA/$26.95 Canada
PROCOMM PLUS 2 For Windows® For Dummies®	by Wallace Wang	ISBN: 1-56884-219-2	$19.99 USA/$26.99 Canada
TCP/IP For Dummies®	by Marshall Wilensky & Candace Leiden	ISBN: 1-56884-241-4	$19.99 USA/$26.99 Canada

For scholastic requests & educational orders please call Educational Sales at 1. 800. 434. 2086

FOR MORE INFO OR TO ORDER, PLEASE CALL ▶ 800 762 2974

For volume discounts & special orders please call Tony Real, Special Sales, at 415. 655. 3048

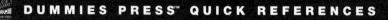